World Scientific Series in Digital Forensics and Cybersecurity - Vol.1

SecureCSocial:
Secure Cloud-Based Social Network

World Scientific Series in Digital Forensics and Cybersecurity

Print ISSN: 2661-4278
Online ISSN: 2661-4286

Series Editor: Sanjay Goel, *The State University of New York at Albany*

This book series covers the latest research in the field of digital forensics as well as the state-of-the-art practice in the field. Eminent researchers and practitioners have been selected to work on different volumes of the series that will be announced and released in a sequence.

Vol. 1   *SecureCSocial: Secure Cloud-Based Social Network*
         by Pradeep K Atrey and Kasun Senevirathna

World Scientific Series in Digital Forensics and Cybersecurity - Vol.1

SecureCSocial:
Secure Cloud-Based Social Network

Pradeep K Atrey
University at Albany, USA

Kasun Senevirathna
University of Winnipeg, Canada

W⊜ World Scientific

NEW JERSEY · LONDON · SINGAPORE · BEIJING · SHANGHAI · HONG KONG · TAIPEI · CHENNAI · TOKYO

Published by

World Scientific Publishing Co. Pte. Ltd.

5 Toh Tuck Link, Singapore 596224

USA office: 27 Warren Street, Suite 401-402, Hackensack, NJ 07601

UK office: 57 Shelton Street, Covent Garden, London WC2H 9HE

Library of Congress Cataloging-in-Publication Data

Names: Atrey, Pradeep K., author.

Title: SecureCSocial: Secure Cloud-Based Social Network / Pradeep K Atrey
(University at Albany, USA) and Kasun Senevirathna (University of Winnipeg, Canada)

Description: New Jersey : World Scientific, [2019] | Series: World Scientific Series in Digital
Forensics and Cybersecurity; vol. 1 | Includes bibliographical references and index.

Identifiers: LCCN 2019018483 | ISBN 9789811205910 (hc)

Subjects: LCSH: Computer networks--Security measures. | Online social networks--
Security measures. | Computer network architectures.

Classification: LCC TK5105.59 .A88 2019 | DDC 384.3/8--dc23

LC record available at https://lccn.loc.gov/2019018483

British Library Cataloguing-in-Publication Data

A catalogue record for this book is available from the British Library.

For any available supplementary material, please visit
https://www.worldscientific.com/worldscibooks/10.1142/11433#t=suppl

Desk Editors: Anthony Alexander/Yu Shan Tay

Typeset by Stallion Press
Email: enquiries@stallionpress.com

Dedication

To my mother: Sumitra Devi,
wife: Manisha Atrey, and
children: Akanksha and Pranjal
— Pradeep K. Atrey

To my parents: Percy and Amara Senevirathna,
wife: Ruvini Senevirathna, and
children: Sahas, Siyansa and Savik
— Kasun Senevirathna

Preface

The use of online social networks (OSNs) has grown exponentially in recent years, and these networks continue to have an ever-increasing impact on human lives. One important fact that OSN users overlook is the potential of the social network operator (SNO) itself becoming an adversary to their privacy. It is observed that most OSN users place absolute faith in SNOs which are mostly profit-oriented entities. As a profit-creating mechanism, these SNOs might share user information with third parties. Further, it is a known fact that SNOs share user information with third party application developers to build applications within their OSNs. Even the SNO might not be able to guarantee the privacy of users when such information is shared with third parties.

Privacy is a subjective measure and it can be difficult to be defined, particularly in an OSN environment. But at a minimum we can assume that the users expect their data being observed by intended parties only. There have also been certain concerns that SNOs may keep user data even after users delete them from their accounts (or delete the accounts themselves), and the SNO may provide a false assurance to the user about the deletion of the posted data.

In order to address these concerns, this book makes a contribution toward proposing a new architecture for online social networking, called SecureCSocial, based on distributed cloud-based datacenters. Specifically, it uses Shamir's Secret Sharing (SSS) as the method of encrypting users' data for enhanced privacy and availability. The book is organized into three parts. The first part focuses on Understanding Security and Privacy Issues in OSNs, the second one presents the Network Architecture and Functions of the SecureCSocial, and the third one describes its Prototype Implementation and Analysis of the SecureCSocial. We conclude the book with a summary of the contributions made as well as the many remaining challenges and directions for future work.

Part I introduces with the security and privacy issues in current OSNs and includes two chapters. The first chapter presents an introduction to the security and privacy issues associated with the current OSNs and motivates the need of a secure OSN. The second chapter reviews the security and privacy mechanisms that are in practice in the current OSNs and also discusses recent efforts in enhancing the security and privacy in OSNs.

Part II describes the Fundamental Network Architecture and Other Preliminaries of the SecureCSocial and includes two chapters. The first chapter in this part presents the essential building blocks of the proposed secure and privacy-aware OSN along with other preliminaries such as cloud datacenter-based decentralization and securing user profiles using SSS. The next chapter zooms into the primary operations and secondary functionalities that are supported by the proposed OSN.

Part III focuses on the Prototype Implementation and Analysis of the SecureCSocial. It includes three chapters and starts with a security analysis of the proposed OSN from many perspectives including choice of SSS and vulnerability against different potential adversaries. In addition, different primary operations and secondary functionalities of the proposed OSN are analyzed for security as per the security standard services. The next chapter describes the implementation of the proof of concept and analyzes the feasibility, performance, and scalability of the proposed OSN. The last chapter provides a summary of the contributions of this book and discusses the many open challenges in this important research area.

This book serves two primary purposes. One, it provides OSN users a better sense of their privacy in the existing OSNs. Second, researchers and industry professionals working in the areas ranging from security and privacy to social media can use this book as a reference text to design and develop an OSN that provides users improved security and privacy. Clearly, the proposed secure OSN has many limitations which need to be resolved in future. There exist multiple opportunities to enhance and improve the proposed OSN to add more functionalities that the existing OSNs possess.

About the Authors

Pradeep K. Atrey is an Associate Professor at the State University of New York, Albany, NY, USA. He is also the Director of the computer science undergraduate program and the founding co-Director of the Albany Lab for Privacy and Security (ALPS). His current research interests are in the area of security and privacy with a focus on multimedia surveillance and privacy, multimedia security, secure-domain cloud-based large-scale multimedia analytics, and social media. He has authored/co-authored over 130 research articles at reputed ACM, IEEE, and Springer journals and conferences. Dr. Atrey is on the editorial board of several journals including *ACM Transactions on Multimedia Computing, Communications and Applications* (*TOMM*), Elsevier's *Signal Processing: Image Communication*, and *ETRI Journal* published by Wiley. He has been associated with over 60 international conferences/workshops in various roles such as General Chair, Program Chair, Area Chair, Publicity Chair, Web Chair, Demo Chair, and TPC Member. Atrey was a recipient of several awards, including the *ACM TOMM* Associate Editor of the Year (2015), the *IEEE Comm. Soc. MMTC* Best R-Letter Editor Award (2015), the Erica and Arnold Rogers Award for Excellence in Research and Scholarship (2014), *ETRI Journal* Best Editor Award (2012), and *ETRI Journal* Best Reviewer Award

(2009). He was also recognized as the ACM Multimedia Rising Star (2015), the ICME Outstanding Organizing Committee Member (as Publicity Chair) (2013), and the ICME Quality Reviewer (2011).

Kasun Senevirathna is currently working as an Information Systems Business Analyst for the Winnipeg Police Service. He graduated from The University of Winnipeg with a master's degree in Applied Computer Science and also holds an MBA in Management of Technology and a BSc in Electronics and Telecommunication Engineering from The University of Moratuwa, Sri Lanka. Kasun has worked as a researcher and a professional in the domains of information security and privacy, data networks, wireless broadband networks, and project management.

Acknowledgments

The credit of this book goes to Kasun Senevirathna, who consolidated upon this vague but ambitious idea of having a cloud-based secure online social network (SecureCSocial). In addition, Taylor Budzan also deserves thanks for helping in the development of the SecureC-Social. I am also thankful to all my colleagues who have supported me in this research at different stages.

— Pradeep K. Atrey

I wish to express the deepest appreciation to my co-author, Pradeep K. Atrey, for providing guidance and direction from the very first day. He continually offered his guidance and shared his knowledge and experience, and was a real pleasure to work with. Besides my advisor, I would like to thank Taylor Budzan for all his support in the implementation of the proof of concept. Last but not the least, I would like to thank my wife Ruvini Senevirathna, for all the dedication and commitment she had to bear with me in completion of this book.

— Kasun Senevirathna

Contents

Acronyms

ABE   Attribute-based Encryption
ASCII   American Standard Code for Information Interchange
CA   Certificate Authority
CDC   Cloud Datacenter
CRL   Certificate Revocation List
DAC   Discretionary Access Control
DB   Database
DCT   Discrete Cosine Transform
DHT   Distributed Hash Table
DNS   Domain Name System
DoS   Denial of Service
GF   Galois Field
GK   Gatekeeper
GMT   Greenwich Mean Time
GUI   Graphical User Interface
HTTPS   Hyper Text Transfer Protocol Secure
IaaS   Infrastructure as a Service
ISP   Internet Service Provider
IT   Information Technology
OSN   Online Social Network
PaaS   Platform as a Service
PKC   Public Key Cryptography
PKI   Public Key Infrastructure
SaaS   Software as a Service
SHA   Secure Hash Algorithm

SN	Social Network
SNO	Social Network Operator
SQL	Structured Query Language
SSL	Secure Socket Layer
SSS	Shamir's Secret Sharing
TCP/IP	Transmission Control Protocol/Internet Protocol
TLS	Transport Layer Security
VPS	Virtual Private Server
XML	Extensible Markup Language

Part I

Understanding Security and Privacy Issues in Online Social Networks

Chapter 1

Introduction

Online Social Networks (OSNs) are one of the most prominent developments the world has observed in the past decade. However, the concept is not totally novel [46]. For example, the use of emails for communication is a form of online social networking. The magnitude of usage and the spectrum of applications that are supported in today's OSNs make them stand out from the individual social networking applications that were prevalent for quite some time, such as emails and instant messaging. An OSN is essentially a network (a computer hardware and software system) which models the real social networks (SNs) that exist naturally in the world. Hence, an OSN consists of users, connections, communications, and data shared by users. Users can be individuals or organizations.

An OSN can be a large repository of multimedia data, some of which is highly sensitive to user privacy. Today's OSNs are not just restricted to building and maintaining real life SNs in an online form. In addition, they act as an application service and a communication service [21]. OSNs are usually web-based and they almost never perfectly match the underlying SN they are trying to model. Most of the OSNs today follow the client server architecture that may not really match the actual natural SNs in the real world.

Therefore, in the research presented in this book, we try to solve this disconnect between OSNs and real life SNs by proposing a decentralized architecture that also provides higher security and privacy for OSN users. Such a study has become essential due to the strong positive influences OSNs have exhibited on real life SNs, the ever increasing number of violations of privacy of users in OSN environments, and the questionable behavior of certain Social Network Operators (SNOs). In summary, we want to find a solution to overcome the privacy threats that exist in today's OSNs, while making sure society still benefits from the services of OSNs.

1.1   Overview of OSNs and User Behavior in OSNs

OSNs have a significant impact on most of the people around the globe who are computer literate. OSNs like Facebook©, Twitter©, and LinkedIn© are attracting more users each day and the networks themselves are evolving and adding more and more features. Some common functionalities that can be observed in today's OSNs include searching for friends/contacts, sharing information and content, commenting on shared content, news feeds, and instant messaging. An OSN can be open or closed, depending on its availability [4]. If the OSN is equally available to anyone globally who has access to the Internet, then it is an open OSN. These are generally the ones people are most familiar with. But there exist OSNs that have restricted user bases such as intranets within organizations. In this study, we only focus on open OSNs as we believe that in closed OSNs, the privacy threats to users are minimal, and refer to open OSNs whenever we use the term OSN.

An average user tends to share more information in an OSN environment than they are required to maintain social interactions [9]. Privacy related information of a user in an OSN can generally be categorized into five broader categories based on the observations of existing OSNs. They are thumbnail, greater profile, list of friends, user-generated content, and comments [9]. Also, on a much broader level, the core information and data generated, maintained, and shared by users in a typical OSN can be classified as follows [21]:

- **Personal contact details:** Describes "who the user is". Includes user's name, gender, picture, birthday, birth place, email address, phone number, current city of living, and other attributes to uniquely identify a user.

- **Information:** Describes "whom the user knows". It is generally the user's contact list. It also describes "what the user likes and is interested in", such as personal interests, hobbies, and preferences (music styles, favorite movies, and sexual, religious, and political views).
- **Information on the curriculum vitae:** Describes the "professional career and educational background" of the user. Includes schools, high schools, colleges, universities the user attended, the qualifications achieved by the user, employers the user has worked for, and the job functions he has carried out.
- **Communication:** Describes "which messages have been exchanged with which users". Includes direct communications like messaging and indirect communications such as "poking" and "likeness tests".

Because OSNs have become huge repositories of privacy sensitive data of real-world individuals and organizations, they have become lucrative targets of adversaries for various reasons. Due to this reason, OSNs allow users to have control over their privacy by providing several privacy control settings. Generally OSN users can control the following [24]:

- The visibility of the online presence within the OSN.
- The visibility of contacts from the user's contact lists.
- The visibility and access to his own profile information.
- The accessibility to his own uploaded content and posted communications.
- The ability to search the user's profile within the OSN.

However, OSNs provide permissive default privacy settings such that viewing privileges are allowed to more users than just friends. So unless a user explicitly adjusts his privacy settings, he does not control who is accessing his information published in the OSN.

Third-party adversaries are only a part of the story. Adversaries can be of any form, from an external unknown third party to the user to the SNO itself. The privacy threat posed by the SNOs is generally given less consideration, mainly because most OSN users instinctively have faith in the SNO. Therefore, in this study, we try to decouple the storage of user profile data from other services in the OSN, and effectively eliminate the need for the role of an SNO. We believe that public, commercial grade cloud datacenters are a good platform for distributed secure storage of user profiles in the proposed OSN, due to high reliability, availability, and security. The next section provides an overview of the concept of cloud computing and an introduction to cloud datacenters.

1.2   Overview of Cloud Computing and Cloud Datacenters

Cloud computing is all about sharing computing resources among a large community. Peter Mell and Tim Grance of the National Institute of Standards and Technology (NIST) Information Technology Laboratory define cloud computing as follows [12]:

Cloud computing is a model for enabling convenient, on-demand network access to a shared pool of configurable and reliable computing resources (e.g., networks, servers, storage, applications, services) that can be rapidly provisioned and released with minimal consumer management effort or service provider interaction. This cloud model promotes availability and is composed of five essential characteristics, three service models, and four deployment models.

The five characteristics of cloud computing as mentioned in the above definition are as follows:

- **Broad network access:** The cloud should be accessible by multiple device types such as laptops, workstations, mobile phones, and thin clients.
- **On-demand self-service:** The cloud service should support self-provisioning.

- **Resource pooling:** Computing, network, and storage resources are pooled and shared among different users in a cloud enviornment.
- **Measured service:** The consumption of the pooled resources is to be monitored and reported to the user/consumer to provide an overview of rates of consumption and associated costs.
- **Rapid elasticity:** The capability to provision and deprovision resources in a short span of time is a critical cost-saving characterstic of cloud computing when compared to legacy systems.

Cloud computing services are provided in three service models as follows:

- **Software as a Service (SaaS):** The cloud service provider gives accessibility to software applications run on the cloud to its users.
- **Platform as a Service (PaaS):** In this service model, the cloud provides a development environment to design, test, and deploy new applications. It also provides middleware-style services such as database and component services that can be used by applications.
- **Infrastructure as a Service (IaaS):** The necessary hardware resources to run a user software application are provided by the cloud service provider. Such hardware resources include processing hardware, storage, networking, and other fundamental computing resources.

The four deployment models for the cloud as mentioned in the above definition are listed as follows:

- **Private cloud:** A cloud service built and designed for a single user to support user specific functions. Not accessible by the public.
- **Community cloud:** More than one group sharing a common specific need as a community generally access the cloud service. Again not to be accessed by the general public.
- **Public cloud:** The most widely known deployment model where users without any common interest/use have access to the cloud service. These services are generally not restricted and are publicly accessible.

- **Hybrid cloud:** A combination of two or more of the above deployment models having a management framework to operate as a single cloud.

Cloud datacenters are usually known to be cloud service providers having a public cloud deployment model and all three service models as described above. They are becoming alternatives for organizations as well as individual users to fulfill their various information technology (IT) requirements and services at lower operational and capital costs, simply because of resource pooling.

1.3   Research Motivation, Goal, Challenges, and Contribution

1.3.1   *Research motivation and goal*

As discussed in Section 1.1, with or without proper thought, users share privacy sensitive data and information in OSNs. Therefore, users' privacy can be at stake, unless it is addressed adequately. Some OSN users are already aware of potential third-party adversaries. SNOs have come up with many features to protect users' privacy from third-party adversaries.

However, when considering the privacy threat model, users have to think beyond the third-party adversaries. Specially, the question of "How trustworthy is the SNO?" is getting more and more attention in the OSN user community. Most OSN users instinctively put faith in the SNO. Certain real-world issues that occurred in the past have raised questions about how safe this assumption is [14]. Another interesting conflict associated with the SNOs is the intellectual property rights of the content that users share in an OSN. For example, Facebook©'s terms of use for its users have a clause that states: "You grant us a non-exclusive, transferable, sub-licensable, royalty-free, worldwide license to use any IP content that you post on or in connection with Facebook (IP License). This IP License ends when you delete your IP content or your account unless your content has been shared with others, and they have not deleted it" [2].[1]

In summary, our argument is that users cannot trust SNOs for user privacy and to safekeep the intellectual property rights of the content they share in OSNs. Nevertheless, as mentioned earlier, OSNs add value to efficiently maintaining real-world SNs in an online environment. Hence, there is a need for a secure OSN that trusts only the user's approved contacts (friends), but no one else. This will ensure that users can still benefit from OSNs without risking their privacy. This is the problem we are trying to solve in this study.

1.3.2 *Research challenges*

The main challenge here is to provide at least the basic functionality provided by current OSNs, while not relying on a centralized SNO to safeguard user security and privacy. It is also critical that a mechanism is in place to support universal and anytime accessibility to user profiles by users' contacts. A naïve solution to address this problem could be to encrypt user profiles in existing OSNs and then share the access credentials with user contacts [28], [31]. However, the major limitation here would be a conflict of interests between the SNO and the user. There are studies proposing alternative architectures for OSNs. Some of these studies follow the centralized nature of existing OSNs [17] while others believe centralization is a major risk and propose completely decentralized architectures [6], [24], [34], [41], [43], [45]. These proposals suffer from the weakness of difficulty in supporting irreversible contacts, i.e. removing a friend from the contact list would necessitate re-encryption of the user profile with a new key, and then redistribution of the new key to other existing contacts. Furthermore, maintaining the availability of a user profile to be accessed by his contacts anytime can become an issue in

---

[1] This is the only instance in this work where the term "IP" refers to Intellectual Property. Otherwise, IP always refers to Internet Protocol in this book.

the previously proposed decentralized architectures for OSNs. These limitations are discussed in detail in Chapter 2.

1.3.3 *Contributions*

To overcome the above mentioned problems, in this study we propose a hybrid architecture for OSNs; we call it "SecureCSocial". In the proposed system, most of the functionality of the OSN is decentralized, while some centralization is required to achieve universal indexing and advertising of users. The core idea in our solution is using cryptographic secret-sharing schemes for multimedia, along with private user data storage in cloud-based commercial datacenters.

The novelty of the proposed method lies in using multimedia secret sharing in an OSN context to provide higher security and privacy to users. To the best of our knowledge, this is the first study that uses Shamir's secret sharing [7] to securely store user profiles in an OSN environment and that discusses its feasibility as well. This is the first study that considers a decentralized architecture for OSNs that covers how it can achieve all the basic operations and other important secondary functionalities in the context of an OSN. The contribution of this study can be summarized as follows:

A **decentralized architecture** for online social networking that

- uses **commercial grade public cloud datacenters** to store user profiles using **Shamir's secret sharing** as the encryption mechanism, thus providing **information theoretic security** to the data stored as user profiles in the OSN;
- presents its feasibility in providing all the **basic operations** in an OSN along with other **important secondary functionalities**;
- has a trust model that considers a user's **friends/contacts as the only trusted parties** from a user's perspective, therefore incorporating security mechanisms to secure user privacy from all other entities in the OSN environment;
- discusses its **resource requirements, user experience** and trade-off in **processing time**.

1.4 Outline of the Book

The rest of the book is organized as follows:

- Chapter 2 explores past works on the subject of security and privacy in OSNs, focusing more on different solutions that have been proposed in different studies. It also presents the fundamental concept of Shamir's secret sharing, followed by its application to encrypt multimedia content.
- Chapter 3 presents the overall network architecture of the proposed OSN with all of its major components and explains how they interact in the OSN.
- Chapter 4 describes how to implement basic operations and some important secondary functions of a typical OSN in the proposed architecture.
- Chapter 5 analyzes the proposed OSN architecture for its security and vulnerability of user privacy, and evaluates different security mechanisms deployed in the system to achieve the proposed trust model, i.e. only the user's friends are trusted in the OSN.
- Chapter 6 presents details of a proof of concept implementation of the proposed solution along with a discussion of the proposed OSN architecture's performance and scalability.
- Chapter 7 summarizes and concludes the book. It also sheds some light on potential improvements and optimizations, and other prospects of the proposed architecture as future research directions.

Chapter 2

Background and Related Work

Security and privacy in OSNs have been the subject of many studies in the past, focusing on different aspects of a much broader problem. Most of them still try to enhance user security against third-party adversaries, while some emphasize the need for more privacy when SNOs are considered as adversaries. First we will focus on different types of attacks in an OSN in Section 2.1, as discussed in [21]. Then attention is paid to efforts to preserve user privacy in existing OSNs in Section 2.2. It is becoming more common to see alternative architectures being proposed to overcome the inherent privacy weaknesses in existing OSN architectures. Section 2.3 presents a survey of such diverse architectures proposed for online social networking to enhance user privacy with Sections 2.3.1 and 2.3.2 dedicated to centralized alternative architectures and decentralized alternative architectures, respectively. Shamir's secret sharing being the main encryption algorithm used to store user profiles in the proposed OSN, its basic concepts are reviewed in Section 2.4, followed by studies done on its application in multimedia (text, images, and video) encryption.

2.1 Security and Privacy Threats in OSNs

Cutillo *et al.* [21] present a spectrum of attacks that are common in OSN environments and their malicious intentions. They are listed and explained as follows:

- **Fake profiles and Sybil attacks:** Nonusers as well as valid users in an OSN may create fake profiles for sinister purposes. The ability to create fake profiles is mainly due to the lack of proper authentication at the user registration phase. The creation of fake profiles paves the path to Sybil attacks, where fake account owners try to connect with OSN users for the purpose of acquiring privacy sensitive information.

- **Plain impersonation:** This is a special type of fake profiles where the adversary aims to create fake profiles only for real-world individual/organizations. The prevention of this type of attacks strongly depends on the thoroughness of the user authentication/ verification mechanisms that are deployed when users get registered with an OSN, and how much accurate information the attacker can access about the targeted individual.

- **Profile cloning:** This is a special type of impersonation attack that occurs within the same OSN. Here, the adversary is creating a profile pretending to be a user who has already subscribed to that OSN and is in possession of a valid profile in the OSN.

- **Profile hijacking:** The goal of the attacker is to obtain control of one or more existing profiles in an OSN. Even though user profiles are secured in almost all the OSNs using passwords, these types of attacks are not uncommon due to many vulnerabilities such as weak passwords.

- **Profile porting:** This is another special type of impersonation attack. The adversary creates a profile for another individual in an OSN by importing valid profile information about the target user from another OSN, where the target individual is already a registered user. Plain impersonation, profile cloning, profile hijacking, and profile porting are collectively termed and grouped as "ID theft" attacks.

- **Profiling:** Attackers collect information about a user in an OSN environment through his profile and information postings. The collected information might be used for a sinister purpose in real life.

- **Secondary data collection:** Going beyond profiling, an attacker collects more information about the targeted user from secondary information sources. This can be considered to be the second phase of a profiling attack.

- **Fake requests:** An attacker, who already has an account in the OSN (may be a fake account), sends fake friend requests targeting certain users. Targeted users tend to accept fake friend requests. Accepted fake requests from an attacker can be the doorway to many attacks.

- **Crawling and harvesting:** The goal of a crawling attack is to collect and aggregate publicly available information across multiple OSN profiles in an automated way. Unlike profiling, this attack does not target a particular user. Also, this differs from secondary data collection because the sources for information collection are restricted only to OSNs. Crawling results in large datasets with large amounts of private information about OSN users, which is termed as "harvesting". Harvested data can be misused by adversaries for different purposes like selling it to marketing agencies.

- **Image retrieval and analysis:** This type of attack targets multimedia data that users share in OSNs including video. Strong analysis of such data can result in violation of privacy of users by exposing information that the users do not intend to divulge, including information about individuals who are not even users of that OSN.

- **Communication tracking:** This type of attack aims to reveal information about the communications of an OSN user. This type of information may reveal more about a user than the user's profile reveals. This type of an attack may be performed as an advanced level of a profiling attack.

- **Ballot stuffing:** An attacker tries to increase the public interest of a particular entity, event, or incident. This attacker may have other hidden motives, such as making a user uncomfortable in real life or attempting to prompt a Denial of Service attack against the SNO.

- **Defamation:** This attack aims to decrease the public's positive interest in an entity. Examples of such an attack may include tarnishing the reputation of a user and conducting anti-advertising campaigns against companies.

- **Censorship:** The attacker has the ability to modify or block certain data that gets published or transferred in an OSN. The SNO and group moderators are potential censors in an OSN environment.

- **Collusion attacks:** Several adversaries join their malicious activities in order to affect OSN users or attack against the OSN applications or the OSN platform itself. All the attacks discussed above can be performed as a collusion attack. Therefore, a collusion attack is more of a method to perform attacks by adversaries in an OSN environment.

2.2 Protecting User Privacy in Conventional OSNs

There are already multiple OSNs operating today. Some of them are global while some are regional. They have attracted billions of users. Some single OSNs have millions of users, which means that there is a high level of acceptance of these OSNs and large investments are being made by SNOs as well. Therefore, considering the potential room for improvement against potential attacks and privacy risks in OSNs, there have been several studies focusing on how to improve user security and privacy in existing OSN environments.

Since a very high number of users just keep the default privacy settings provided by the OSNs, it is prudent to study a default privacy policy for OSN users that minimizes privacy leakage without hindering the expected general functionalities of the OSN. A machine language approach is proposed in [15] that analyzes sufficiently large samples of existing privacy policies of OSN users to produce default privacy policies that have higher probabilities of being accepted by new users. The proposed method, called the "collaborative analysis process", is comprised of three steps. They are calculating the similarity between policies, clustering policies, and personalizing policy selection. The similarity between two policies is determined by the different properties of the policies such as the social groups, location restrictions, and time restrictions. Once similarities between policies are determined, then they are to be grouped into clusters to find a varied set of distinct policies. Finally, the policies from the clusters relevant to a user are personalized as suggestions.

There is a conflict of interest between social networking goals and the privacy of users. Generally, community building is one of the prime goals for a user of an OSN. Trying to protect privacy may adversely affect to that goal. Staddon [19] considers LinkedIn© as a case study and proves his argument using a method for discovering LinkedIn© contacts, which are supposed to be hidden based on their privacy settings (This study was done in 2009 and this vulnerability may have already been addressed by LinkedIn© by now). More research efforts need to focus on efficient methods for detecting privacy breaches in OSNs and on building user awareness of privacy risks and the trade-off between privacy and utility in OSNs. Two areas of further research are proposed in [19], addressing this requirement. First, in privacy-oriented modeling and analysis, it might be possible to construct a skeleton model of an OSN, because today's OSNs share similar features. This skeleton can be extended to capture additional services of an OSN. Then, this skeleton can be formally analyzed to identify potential privacy breaches. However, failure to model attacks that rely on outside information is a limitation and an area for further research. The second suggested approach is data mining-driven privacy metrics. Even though certain privacy sensitive information such as friends of a user is not directly given, there is a possibility of finding it using data mining techniques as [19] has done in the LinkedIn© case study. Most of the privacy breaches in OSN environments have a data mining aspect such as mining of user profiles. The major goals of these techniques are to calibrate the difficulty of a privacy attack or leakage in an effective way and to communicate the associated risks to users, and probably to the SNOs as well. So either the user or the SNO or both can take necessary actions to avoid that risk.

Lucas and Borisov [28] have come up with a solution for protecting information published on Facebook© through encryption. As in most of the cases, the trade-off between the level of security and usability is present in this solution. However, the study tries to strike a balance between the two competing ends, as claimed by the authors. While the authors still believe there could be a potential active attack by the SNO (i.e. Facebook©) on the encrypted information, they claim the proposed architecture dramatically raises the cost of such an attack. They also argue that Facebook© will be placed within a framework for legal privacy protection because such an attack would violate a user's reasonable expectation of privacy. The authors believe the centralized architecture supported by conventional OSNs such as Facebook© has an edge over decentralized OSN versions. Centralized OSNs are ubiquitous, already have large established user bases with an infrastructure already invested in and provide good usability by not exposing network level details and other technical details to the end user.

The same study has built a prototype Facebook© application, named "flyByNight", implementing the proposed architecture, and addressing some of the limitations of the Facebook© platform through proxy cryptography. The main design goals for flyByNight were protecting personal information transmitted to Facebook© using encryption, ensuring Facebook© cannot store plaintext data and/or private key material (hence, plaintext data does not appear on the Internet), supporting one-to-one and one-to-many communications, and using Facebook© for key management purposes as well. The proposed architecture involves a third-party application server to run the flyByNight application and to keep a message database. The client-side JavaScript application handles the key generation and other cryptographic operations. These operations were realized using open source JavaScript implementations of AES and RSA, and El Gamal implementation on top of the math routines in RSA. The need for the El Gamal algorithm has risen as a result of the very large amount of time taken to generate the keys in the RSA algorithm by the restricted JavaScript architecture. However, this carries the trade-off of having slower encryption and decryption compared to using RSA.

The implemented prototype application was unable to achieve encryption of images and posted videos. The authors state that it would have been desirable to encrypt the images posted in Facebook©, since images themselves carry very important information related to the privacy of users, but the JavaScript architecture makes achieving this goal quite difficult. Furthermore, the requirement for a third-party application server to run the flyByNight application and to store messages exchanged between users poses the question of who will provide such a service and what would be the incentives to do so. The trustworthiness of the application server provider needs to be clarified. Otherwise, the confidentiality of the whole architecture relies on the protection provided by the passwords users use to encrypt their private keys in the public-key infrastructure (PKI) architecture. Nonetheless, this study claims that the design and the implementation of the prototype application have addressed several usability concerns that are important. The universal accessibility as a web application, no significant effect on the performance of the Facebook© site as perceived by the end user, and the expectation of less technical knowledge from the end user to execute the developed application were the usability concerns that were considered when developing flyByNight.

NOYB [42] is an approach that can be implemented on existing OSNs to provide better user privacy while preserving some of the functionalities in the OSN. NOYB relies on the fact that OSNs can operate on "fake" data. It does not necessarily require the cooperation of the SNO, as the SNOs are considered as untrusted entities. The three main design goals for NOYB are privacy preservation, incremental deployability, and difficult detection (by the SNO and other adversaries). While the authors have implemented a proof of concept version of NOYB in Facebook©, NOYB inherits some basic limitations. First, using fake data on user profiles completely hinders the capability to search for a friend who uses NOYB. Secondly, NOYB does not address security and privacy in the context of photos and videos. The implementation of other important functionalities in an OSN such as messaging and commenting on shared content is not straightforward in NOYB (especially how they can be protected from the untrusted SNO). Also, maintaining a dictionary to swap actual atomic data with fake data is challenging. Most importantly, NOYB lacks the flexibility to remove friends from a user's contact list, since it would mean encrypting user profile again with a new key and sharing the new key with other friends. That requirement reduces the system's flexibility to a large extent. NOYB may be appropriate for a well-coordinated small group, but not on an individual basis in a relatively large OSN.

Atrey [31] has proposed a secret-sharing-based key management scheme for encrypting the users' data in order to preserve their privacy in OSN environments. Secret sharing is accepted to be an unconditionally secure method to be used for securing computer related data, including text, images, and videos. Hence, the proposed scheme in [31] for user privacy in OSNs, using secret-sharing-based key management is argued to be unconditionally secure, and also to be computationally efficient. Generally, a (k, n) secret-sharing scheme $(2 \leq k \leq n)$ suggests that there would be n number of shares of the original secret data, and at least k number of shares would be required to reveal the original secret. The threshold scheme for secret sharing in [31] is $(2, n)$, where n can be an integer value sufficiently larger than the number of current friends for a particular OSN user. The value for n being larger than the number of current friends provides additional space for future friends of that particular user. In this architecture, users of a particular OSN would use a social networking client application that is responsible for four main tasks: key share generation, key reconstruction, distribution and receiving of key shares using a public–private key mechanism, and data encryption. The transfer of all messages and key shares takes place through the SNO in the encrypted form, so that they remain concealed from the SNO. The main drawback in this scheme is that while considering the SNO to be untrustworthy and keeping user data concealed even from the SNO, it still requires the assistance of the SNOs to implement it, which is highly unlikely. There is room for further study on how to implement this scheme without the support of the SNOs while maintaining unconditional security for the keys.

2.3   Recent Alternative Architectures for OSNs to Enhance User Privacy

Based on the reasoning that existing OSNs do not have adequate space to provide sufficient security and privacy and the potential of the SNO itself becoming an adversary, there have been multiple studies trying to create a new OSN architecture that would provide a higher level of security and user privacy. There have been studies proposing diverse-architectures for privacy-sensitive OSNs, but still adopting the conventional client–server model. On the other hand, believing the centralized client–server model itself is the main vulnerability in an OSN, many studies have proposed and implemented decentralized OSN architectures, emulating actual real-world SNs.

2.3.1   *Centralized client–server architectures*

In [17], Anderson *et al.* have proposed an architecture for OSNs that builds an OSN out of smart clients and an untrusted central server. It is intended to protect users' privacy information from both the operator of the OSN and other network users. Therefore, it removes the need for faith in the SNO and is expected to give users control of their privacy. This proposed client–server-based architecture supports the following five basic functionalities at a minimum, as claimed by the authors. They are:

- **Extensibility:** The proposed architecture supports third-party applications to be installed and run as users wish, without yielding control of user privacy information to the application provider. A social API is provided along with this architecture.
- **Social links:** The architecture must be able to create social interactions in the OSN, among real life social links. It is important

that other nodes the user connects to are verified from fake users to ensure user privacy is preserved from threats such as phishing attacks.

- **Posting personal information:** The ability to post personal information and protect it from adversaries is essential. Since the SNO is untrustworthy, access control should be done at the client level.
- **Messaging:** The proposed architecture must have the ability to send and receive messages between connected users confidentially, while preserving integrity of messages.
- **Joint content:** The architecture must be able to publish content that is common to more than one user in the OSN.

In this architecture, the server resides as a hub, is not trustworthy, and provides only the availability. The clients must be smart and are responsible for the confidentiality and integrity of their own operations and data. The storage provider does not have to provide the client software. The client software can be provided by multiple competing vendors who adhere to certain specifications. This overall architecture is relatively secure, but there is still the risk of the SNO (operator of the central server) performing traffic analysis and becoming a potential threat to users of the OSN. Further study is required on how access control and authentication mechanisms should be maintained at the central server, especially when friends are removed from a user's contact list.

2.3.2 Decentralized architectures

All the OSNs in operation today are based on centralized architectures. These centralized architectures result in two major risks that can adversely affect the privacy of users [5]. First, a centralized architecture stores all user data in a single administrative domain. This concentration of user data is a vulnerability that can result in large-scale privacy breaches. These privacy breaches can occur due to intentional as well as unintentional data disclosures. Second, centralization is a threat to user data ownership. Most of the SNOs require their users to agree to give license to the SNO to use uploaded content by the users in an OSN, as the SNO wishes. This has a huge potential for copyright violations. Therefore, to overcome these inherent weaknesses of a centralized model, it seems prudent to look for decentralized counterparts.

Irrespective of the underlying network infrastructure, in a decentralized OSN, a user needs to have his own personal server to host his own data. This personal server is termed as Virtual Individual Server (VIS) in [5]. VISs representing users in real life can be self-organized into peer-to-peer overlay networks. While there can be many variations of decentralized OSNs, [5] presents three broad categories based on the VIS placement. First there can be cloud-based decentralization. The VISs are run in paid computing utility environments, i.e. cloud-based datacenters. Second, the decentralization can be desktop-based with socially-informed replication of user data. User data resides primarily in the user's own desktop computer (at home or office). To provide more availability, users can adopt a socially-informed replication scheme, where cleartext data of users can be replicated in trusted VISs. The third variation is to have a hybrid of the above two variations. The user keeps his data in his own desktop server; with a fall back option to a highly-available standby VIS whenever the desktop server becomes unavailable. The standby high availability server can be a paid computing utility server.

Vis-à-Vis [6] is a cloud-based decentralization of an OSN as discussed above, that acts as a proof of concept. Vis-à-Vis is a federation of independent VISs that run on cloud-based paid computing utilities. To represent and create social groups, VISs are self-organized as overlay networks. Vis-à-Vis is implemented with the intention to support location-based OSNs. The concept can be extended to other OSNs as well. A "group" is the central abstraction supported by Vis-à-Vis. Every user in Vis-à-Vis has a public and private key pair that are self-signed. Since the VIS will be acting on behalf of the user, the private key of the key pair is stored securely at his VIS. Users have to distribute their public keys and the connecting IP addresses of their VISs to other users out-of-band. Each group in Vis-à-Vis has an owner (the user who creates the group), member users of the group, and a mapping of group members to geographic regions. The geographic region is the geographic area that a user wishes to share with the other members of the group. It can be fine-grained into a level like GPS coordinates or can be coarse-grained into a level like the country, depending on the user's preference to share his location details with other members. Vis-à-Vis is a strong initiation toward more privacy sensitive decentralized social networks, with high availability. There is much room for further research and improvement. This architecture needs to be further developed without assuming the computing utility datacenter as a trusted party. Removing that assumption may put additional overhead on clients accessing the OSN. However, given the privacy risk and the fact that the processing power of user end devices are increasing, it may prove to be a worthwhile consideration.

Persona [34] is another decentralized OSN that gives more control to users over their data. Users can decide where to store their data (depending on how the users choose the storage service, Persona may have a centralized architecture as well), but rather than trusting the data storage provider, it relies on cryptographic techniques to protect user privacy. Persona uses attribute-based encryption (ABE), traditional public-key cryptography (PKC), and automated key management mechanisms when translating between the two cryptosystems. It is built upon two abstract goals: To hide personal information from aggregators and to hide personal information from colleagues, as appropriate. Each Persona user creates two keys, a private key and a public key, using the public-key cryptosystem. The public key is distributed among friends out-of-band. A Persona user can create groups of friends and control which group has access to which data by encrypting data to groups. To achieve these goals, a traditional approach combining symmetric and asymmetric cryptography could have been used. However, the traditional cryptography gives less flexibility, e.g. when encryption is required for a group that is not specifically defined, but is an intersection of two already defined groups. ABE provides more flexibility than traditional cryptosystems.

Onc of the major limitations of Persona occurs when a user is removed from a group. This leads to re-keying, where all the existing members must be given a new key.

Safebook [22–26] is a decentralized peer-to-peer architecture for OSNs. The key feature here is that trust relationships inherent in real life SNs are leveraged in order to assure privacy and enforce cooperation among peer nodes. The proposed system consists of three main architectural components. They are:

- **Several matryoshkas:** A matryoshka refers to several rings of nodes based on trust relationships when perceived from a particular user's point of view. There are several concentric rings centered at the user node. The innermost ring consists of the set of nodes that represent the trusted contacts of the user. The next ring consists of trusted contacts of the first inner ring. The rings continue like this based on trust relationships.
- **A peer-to-peer substrate:** A peer-to-peer substrate consists of all the nodes in the OSN. The main objective of the peer-to-peer substrate is to provide data lookup services. A distributed hash table (DHT) can be used as the peer-to-peer substrate. The identity of a peer is revealed only to a trusted contact.
- **A trusted identification service:** The trusted identification service is responsible for providing each node with a unique pseudonym and a node identifier, and the related certificates. It provides resistance against Sybil and impersonation attacks.

Safebook can achieve reasonable availability while ensuring anonymity by having three or four shells (the limitation for anonymity is that the number of shells must be higher than or equal to two). With three shells, a spanning factor of one, and a probability of 0.3 of each node being online, Safebook requires 85 contacts to ensure 90% data availability. When the number of shells increases to four, the same data availability demands 290 hosts. Also, for a spanning factor of two, it requires at least 13 and 23 contacts for three shells and fours shells, respectively, for the same data availability [26]. This is the main limitation in Safebook. To achieve a reasonable level of availability, a user has to share his profile with a high number of peers, which can become a vulnerability since data integrity can be a potential issue.

PrPl is another proposed decentralized architecture for online social networking that claims that users can participate in online social networking without losing data ownership [45]. The main design goals of PrPl are decentralization, openness, and trustworthiness. PrPl is associated with the concept of a "Personal-Cloud Butler", which is a personal service that can be trusted to keep the personal data of users. The Butler can be run on a home server or on a server of a paid or ad-supported vendor. Going further, Seong *et al.* [45] have developed an expressive query language for social-multi databases based on Datalog, called "SociaLite" to assist potential application developers of the presented OSN infrastructure with simple declarative database queries to access the large collection of private data. The major drawback of this architecture is the need for a cloud butler server. The user has to either own a continuously running butler or run it at a third-party vendor. When it is run on a third-party server, the risk of the vendor (or a malicious insider) accessing user information in an unauthorized manner is still present.

PeerSoN [41] is a peer-to-peer decentralized architecture for online social networking, which is designed to enhance user security and privacy. The authors have not considered the encryption of stored data in the OSN (to be considered later), though it is one of the main design choices. The study does not provide in-depth analysis of how the proposed architecture can achieve all the primary operations and other important secondary functionalities, especially when data encryption is present. Therefore, while PeerSoN looks promising, it is too early to be considered as a full scale solution for online social networking.

LotusNet [27] is a proposed framework for online social networking that relies on a peer-to-peer paradigm. In [27], the authors try to tackle the trade-off problem between security, privacy, and services in distributed OSNs by providing the users the possibility to tune their privacy settings through a flexible and fine-grained access control system. DECENT [43] is another recently proposed architecture for OSNs that uses a distributed hash table to store user data. The authors of Cachet [44], a decentralized peer-to-peer-based architecture for OSNs, try to provide enhanced privacy through a combination of design features including DHT for decentralization, cryptography (a hybrid scheme of traditional public-key encryption and ABE) to enforce attribute-based policies, and data representation in terms of objects. All these architectures need further work and/or analysis on how they can achieve a reasonable spectrum of general OSN operations and functionalities.

Senevirathna and Atrey [20] first presented the preliminary idea of the novel architecture that is extended in this book, which proposes to use commercial grade CDCs to store users' profiles after being encrypted using Shamir's secret sharing (SSS).

2.4 Shamir's Secret Sharing

In simple terms, the idea behind secret sharing is creating multiple shares of a secret such that more than a specified number of shares would reveal the secret completely while any number of shares less than the specified number would reveal no information at all about the secret. In other words, as given in [7], let the secret be S, and secret sharing creates n shares $S_1, S_2, \ldots, S_n$, such that

- the knowledge of k or more S_i shares would easily calculate the value of S;
- the knowledge of $k - 1$ or fewer S_i shares provides no information at all about S. In other words, all possible values for S are equally probable.

This idea can be implemented numerically by polynomial interpolation [7]. Given a random polynomial $f(x) = (a_0 + a_1 x + a_2 x^2 + \cdots + a_{k-1} x^{k-1})$ we need at least k number of $(x_i, f(x_i))$ points to reconstruct the polynomial accurately with a 100% probability. So, if we take $S = a_0$ in the polynomial, pick coefficients $a_1, \ldots, a_{k-1}$

randomly and then create n number of shares such that SS is the set of all the shares of the secret S,

then $SS = \{(x_i, f(x_i)); 1 \leq i \leq n\}$.

To reconstruct the polynomial and then accurately derive $S = a_0$ we need at least k number of points. Hence, this secret-sharing scheme is termed as a (k, n) threshold scheme. Also, the x values of shares, i.e. $x_1, \ldots, x_n$ are known to be **identifying indices**. To make the interpolation of coefficients more precise, modular arithmetic can be used instead of real arithmetic [7]. A prime number p is chosen such that $S < p$ and $n < p$. While $a_0 = S$, other coefficients $a_1, a_2, \ldots, a_{k-1}$ are chosen randomly from a uniform distribution of $[0, p)$. The set of shares SS is calculated as per the following equation:

$$f(x) = (a_0 + a_1 x + a_2 x^2 + \cdots + a_{k-1} x^{k-1}) \bmod p \qquad (2.1)$$

The coefficients $a_0, a_1, \ldots, a_{k-1}$ can be derived by any k shares using Lagrange interpolation for the k number of pairs of points as per Equation (2.2). Deriving a_0 would be sufficient since it is the secret value S.

$$g(x) = \left[\sum_{j=1}^{k} \left(f(x_j) \times \prod_{i=1, i \neq j}^{k} \frac{x - x_i}{x_j - x_i} \right) \right] \bmod p \qquad (2.2)$$

Some properties of secret sharing that have proved to be useful are listed as follows [7]:

(1) The size of each share does not exceed the size of the original data.
(2) S_is can be added or deleted dynamically while keeping k fixed as long as the number of S_is available at a particular point of time is more than k.
(3) The SS can be changed from time to time while still keeping S unchanged, just by using a new polynomial to calculate SS with a new set of random coefficients $a_1, a_2, \ldots, a_{k-1}$. Such an exercise significantly enhances the security and secrecy of S.
(4) A hierarchical scheme is possible for SS by having more than one $(x_i, f(x_i))$ pair per share, hence the number of shares required

to reveal the secret value S will depend on the shares being used to do so.

Secret sharing is information theoretically secure. However, there have been alternative versions of secret sharing proposed for higher efficiency, giving up the requirement for information theoretic security while doing so [16]. There have been numerous studies on how the concept of secret sharing can be practically used to encrypt sensitive data including multimedia. We have provided an overview of studies in the following sections that were carried out for applying SSS to different multimedia types.

2.4.1 *Text secret sharing*

Atrey *et al.* [32] proposed a method to use secret sharing directly on the characters of textual data. They presented two methods for performing SSS on textual data. In both methods, the characters need to be converted to their ASCII values first. Secret sharing is actually carried out on these ASCII values. Once the share values are generated, they are converted back to characters as per ASCII encoding. Therefore, in these schemes, secret sharing is done with the finite field of order 127, i.e. $GF(127)$ with the arithmetic operations modulo 127.

In method 1, named SimpleTSS, each ASCII character is considered a secret and Shamir's (k, n) threshold scheme is applied to create n shares. In the polynomial $f(x) = (a_0 + a_1 x + a_2 x^2 + \cdots + a_{k-1} x^{k-1}) \bmod 127$ that is used to create shares, a_0 is the secret ASCII value of the character to be secret shared. Other coefficients $(a_1, a_2, \ldots, a_{k-1}) \leq 127$ are selected randomly. In the reconstruction phase, k shares $(x_1, f(x_1)), (x_2, f(x_2)), \ldots, (x_k, f(x_k))$ are used in Lagrange interpolation to derive $f(x)$. Hence, a_0 is derived, which is the secret ASCII value of the encrypted character. In this method, SSS is implemented character-by-character in the encryption phase and consequently, the reconstruction is also done character-by-character in the decryption phase.

However, SimpleTSS is still vulnerable against frequency-based attacks, especially in character strings or documents having a significant number of characters, unless different identifying indices are used for each character or the set of coefficients for each character encryption is chosen from a uniform random distribution. To overcome this vulnerability, Atrey, *et al.* [32] propose another method named ModifiedTSS. Here, the character string or the document is divided into $k = P/l$ segments, of size l each. Here, P is the total number of characters in the character string or the document. If the number of characters in the last segment is less than l, then it is padded with space characters to make it of length l. The set of k coefficients of $f(x) = (a_0 + a_1 x + a_2 x^2 + \cdots + a_{k-1} x^{k-1}) \bmod 127$ including a_0 is to be taken from the ASCII values of these k segments of text, such that only one character ASCII value from each segment is to be used in a polynomial and that value is not to be used again in another secret-sharing polynomial. Hence, there will be l number of such polynomials with k coefficients. Therefore, each share will only carry l number of ASCII values/characters. The reconstruction process involves using the Lagrange polynomial to derive each $f(x)$ and the corresponding k number of coefficients in it. These k number of coefficients are mapped to characters according to ASCII encoding and placed accordingly in the text document or the character string. The process is repeated for all the l number of polynomials. Although ModifiedTSS is immune to frequency-based attacks, it is not considered to be information theoretically secure as argued in [16].

In the context of an OSN, the character strings can usually be considered to be of relatively shorter lengths, making it difficult to carry out a successful frequency-based attack. Also, it is possible to choose the set of coefficients randomly for each character. Therefore, we believe that both text secret-sharing schemes proposed by Atrey *et al.* [32] are viable options in the proposed OSN architecture, from a security perspective.

2.4.2 *Image secret sharing*

There have been numerous studies on protecting digital images using secret sharing. The most prominent and related ones for this study are [10], [11], [36], [37] and [39].

In [11], the authors proposed a scheme for uncompressed image secret sharing in the spatial domain. Here, secret sharing is done with the finite field of order 251, i.e. $GF(251)$ with the arithmetic operations mod 251. Secret sharing is to be done on the spatial domain pixel values of the image. However, pixel values 251–255 need to be truncated to 250 of the secret image so that none of the pixels (secrets) carry a value greater than 251. After this step, a key is used to generate a permutation sequence to permute the pixels of the secret image. Then, the image is segmented into I/k segments (I is the total number of pixels in the secret image), of size k each (some padding may be required). Secret sharing is done for each segment taking its k number of pixel values as the coefficients of the polynomial $f(x) = (a_0 + a_1 x + a_2 x^2 + \cdots + a_{k-1} x^{k-1})$ mod 251. Hence, there will be I/k number of pixels in each share, with n such shares (assuming a (k, n) threshold scheme). The reconstruction process involves using the Lagrange polynomial to derive each $f(x)$ and the corresponding k coefficients in it. These k coefficients are mapped accordingly in the appropriate segment of the image. The process is repeated for all the I/k number of polynomials. Then it is necessary to apply the inverse-permutation to get the secret image back. For a color image, the same algorithm needs to be applied to each different component separately (e.g. R, G, and B components).

Alharthi and Atrey [37] provide an improvement to the method in [11] to avoid the need for the permutation step. In this method, the image is segmented into k number of sections either horizontally or vertically. The k number of coefficients in the secret-sharing polynomial $f(x)$ as per Equation (2.1) are taken from different k sections such that each pixel value will be used exactly once in a polynomial. Hence, there will be I/k polynomials and n number of share images carrying I/k number of pixels. The reconstruction process is similar to the process explained in [11], except for the need for inverse-permutation and the way the pixel values are mapped into segments. Though this algorithm does not need the extra steps of permutation and inverse-permutation, it makes certain share images (share images created with low identifying index values, i.e. low

x values) unusable since they disclose enough features of the original image for it to become compromised to a certain extent. Alharthi and Atrey suggest a solution to this problem in [36]. In this study, they propose using different identifying indices within the same share image by incrementing it by a fixed amount y in every other polynomial, such that $x = ((x + y) \bmod 251) + 1$. This ensures that not all the resulting pixel values in a share image are created with the same identifying index. Therefore, the preservation of features of the original image in the share images is prevented.

In [10], Lin and Tsai present a scheme of secret sharing based on the Discrete Cosine Transform (DCT) coefficients of an image. Apart from encryption, this mechanism also provides lossy compression as well. Only 10 coefficients of each DCT transform block are preserved and others are discarded. The DC coefficient of each DCT block is used to create a random sequence of nine integers that are used to conceal the actual values of the nine AC coefficients preserved. The DC coefficients of each DCT block are secret shared and thus n share images are created by performing the inverse DCT on n shares. The finite field of order p, i.e. $GF(p)$ with the arithmetic operations mod p, is selected such that p is the nearest prime number larger than the DC coefficient. In each secret-sharing polynomial, the DC value is taken as the a_0 in Equation (2.1). The other coefficients can be selected randomly from the range $[0, p)$. The reconstruction mechanism will reverse the above mentioned steps starting with the reconstruction of the polynomial $f(x)$ using Lagrange interpolation (or just deriving $f(0) = a_0$ would be sufficient in this case).

Secret sharing of images as proposed in [39] proposes performing encryption on the secret image I using stream cipher. Using a seed value, a sequence of pseudorandom numbers are to be generated using a cryptographically secure pseudorandom number generator. In the uncompressed domain, these pseudorandom numbers are to be added to the pixel values, and in the compressed domain, pseudorandom numbers are added to the DCT coefficients. Then, the encrypted image will be partitioned into n fragments using Reed–Solomon error correction. Using SSS as per Equation (2.1), the key used to create the pseudorandom number sequence will be encrypted and n number of shares are created. The prime number p for the finite field of order p, i.e. $GF(p)$ with the arithmetic operations modulo p, can be chosen as a prime number larger than the value of the key. The value of the key will be the a_0 in Equation 2.1. The other coefficients can be selected randomly from the range $[0, p)$. Each share now consists of a segment from the encrypted image and a share of the key value. In decryption, the encrypted image is reconstructed using the Reed–Solomon correction scheme. Then the key value is reconstructed using Lagrange interpolation. By doing so, the random number sequence can be derived that can be used to decrypt the encrypted image correctly by subtracting the random values from the pixel values or the DCT coefficients depending on whether the image is uncompressed or compressed.

All of the above-mentioned secret-sharing schemes have their own merits and demerits when it comes to performance and security. However, when it comes to the particular application of the context of an OSN, they can all be considered to serve adequately (from an average user perspective) and it remains a design option as to which scheme is to be used.

2.4.3   *Video secret sharing*

In [29], the authors use SSS to encrypt videos. However, unlike other schemes explained above this scheme does not intend to create multiple shares of the secret (in this case a secret video) as the output of the encryption. Rather, it merely uses SSS to distribute the strength of the DC coefficient among the AC coefficients in the DCT domain. Therefore, this mechanism is not a fit for the proposed OSN architecture because it requires multiple shares of the secret video to be stored independently in different CDCs.

In [38], the authors proposed their method in [36] for image secret sharing to be extended to video secret sharing. To improve on the total processing required, this scheme counts the number of subsequent frames in which the pixel values are the same (within a threshold). Therefore, in Equation (2.1), the coefficients are taken from a particular frame as pairs. The first coefficient (e.g. a_0) is the pixel value and the second coefficient (e.g. a_1) is the number of occurrences of that pixel value in subsequent frames at the same pixel location. If the value of k is odd in the (k, n) threshold secret-sharing scheme, a random value can be used as the coefficient a_{k-1} $(a_{k-1} < p)$. In the revealing phase, the polynomial $f(x)$ is reconstructed using Lagrange interpolation, which uses k number of shares. Then, the coefficient values of the derived polynomial $f(x)$ are used to reconstruct the video, taking a pair of coefficients at a time.

The above method of video encryption that exploited only the pixel-wise temporal redundancy in the video is identified as the TemporalSVS method in [33]. In [33], Atrey *et al.* extend the work in [38] by exploiting pixel-wise as well as block-wise redundancies in both spatial and temporal dimensions, thereby presenting two more methods for video secret sharing, namely SpatioTemporalSVS and BlockSVS, respectively. The proposed OSN architecture in this study may use any video secret-sharing scheme from these three methods as they create multiple shares to be stored in CDCs as per the core concept of the proposed architecture. However, it is important to note that these methods focus only on uncompressed videos. Future studies on secret sharing of compressed videos would prove crucial for the proposed OSN architecture, given the frequent use of compressed videos in OSNs.

2.5 Summary

The privacy of OSN users is susceptible to numerous threats and attacks in today's OSNs, as listed in [21]. Fake profiles and Sybil attacks, plain impersonation, profile cloning, profile hijacking, profile porting, profiling, secondary data collection, fake requests, crawling and harvesting, image retrieval and analysis, communication tracking, ballot stuffing, defamation, censorship, and collusion attacks are some threats that have been identified in an OSN environment. There have been several studies focusing on how to improve user security and privacy in existing OSN environments, e.g. [15], [19], [28], [31], [42]. Some of these studies consider the SNO as a trusted entity, while others do not. Significant efforts have been put forward by different scholars to come up with new architectures for OSNs, considering SNOs to be untrustworthy. Some studies have proposed conventional client–server-based architectures (e.g. [17]), while many have opted for a totally decentralized architecture (e.g. [6], [26], [27], [34], [41], [43], [44], [45]).

SSS is considered to be an information theoretically secure encryption scheme. A (k, n) threshold secret-sharing scheme, where $k < n$ implies that at least k number of shares are required to reconstruct the original secret out of n number of shares, and $k - 1$ or lesser number of shares would not reveal any information about the secret value at all. There have been numerous studies that have applied the concept of SSS to securely encrypt multimedia data, i.e. text (e.g. [32]), digital images (e.g. [10], [11], [36], [37], [39]), and video (e.g. [29], [33], [38]).

Part II

SecureCSocial: Network Architecture and Functions

Chapter 3

The Fundamental Network Architecture and Other Preliminaries of the Proposed Solution

This chapter presents the fundamental network architecture of the proposed secure and privacy-aware OSN along with other preliminaries. Section 3.1 explains the preliminaries of the proposed work, i.e. cloud datacenter-based decentralization, securing user profiles using SSS, and the essential building blocks of the proposed OSN. Section 3.2 discusses secure communications of the proposed OSN, followed by a discussion on service infrastructure at CDCs in Section 3.3.

3.1 Preliminaries of the Proposed OSN

The privacy risk for users in today's OSN environments lies in centralized storage of user data beyond the full control of users. Therefore, in this study, we try to propose a decentralized architecture for OSNs where users keep the ownership of their personal data while still giving access to their friends. The most common approach for decentralization that has been proposed so far is a peer-to-peer architecture [24], [27], [40], [41], [43], [44]. The main shortcoming inherent in a peer-to-peer architecture for an OSN is the fact that the user has to rely on his own and/or his peers' computing device(s) to keep the OSN profile accessible by all his friends as they demand. We believe that this is highly unreliable as the level of service of peers cannot be guaranteed for an OSN profile that needs continuous availability. Also, data integrity can be compromised if one or more peers act as adversaries.

As a solution, we propose commercial grade cloud datacenters (CDCs) as the repositories of user data in an OSN. This removes the requirement for a central entity who keeps/stores the data of users beyond users' control. In the meantime, commercial grade CDCs are reliable data storage providers to store user profile data in an OSN environment. Also, users are generally protected against intellectual property copyright violations and other security and privacy breaches by the CDC service provider through the prevailing laws and any legal agreements the user and the CDC service provider conclude.

However, rather than relying on the legal framework to safeguard user privacy, we propose SSS-based encryption when users use CDCs to store their data in the OSN environment. While this provides additional security measures on top of the data security mechanisms put in place by the commercial grade CDCs, it also ensures that user privacy is protected from the CDC service provider (and its internal staff). Section 5.1 provides a detailed explanation of the justification of using SSS as the encryption mechanism in the proposed OSN architecture.

Section 2.4 provides the fundamental concepts of SSS and how it can be used as an encryption algorithm, followed by its application in multimedia (text, digital images, and video) encryption. In this proposed architecture, SSS is used as the encryption mechanism before storing user profiles in databases at CDCs. Data shared in an OSN environment is comprised of multimedia, i.e. textual data (e.g. user information), images (e.g. profile picture, photo albums), and videos posted by users. Despite the availability of numerous methods for encrypting a given multimedia-type using SSS as discussed in Section 2.4, the proposed OSN architecture is open to any such scheme. In other words, the proposed architecture can accept the most efficient secret-sharing algorithms as design options.

As explained in Section 2.4, secret sharing used in this architecture is referred to as a (k, n) threshold scheme. While k $(k \geq 2)$

is a design parameter, n ($n \geq k$) depends on the user's preference on how many CDCs he wants to store shares of his OSN profile on. The higher the value of n, the higher the reliability of accessibility of user profile by his friends. While secret sharing is the main encryption scheme for storing data at CDCs, all the communications between different entities within this architecture are secured using public-key-based cryptography and symmetric session-key-based encryption. These security mechanisms will come to light subsequently.

A high-level abstract view of the proposed architecture is shown in Figure 3.1. Here two OSN users (User 1 and User 2) are using three CDCs to store the shares of their OSN profiles. For the sake of simplicity in this example, we have shown that both the users have adopted a (2, 2) threshold scheme for secret sharing. However, this does not have to be the case. Having decided where to store user data and how to store it, the next challenge would be how to build a friend network for a particular user. To address this requirement, we introduce a central server (or multiple servers, theoretically) to maintain a database (DB) of users who have subscribed to the OSN, named the "Advertiser". This is also depicted in Figure 3.1. Also shown in Figure 3.1 is a Certificate Authority (CA) that is imperative in secure communications between different entities with public-key certificates as per the ITU-T X.509 standard [50]. All the entities in the proposed architecture are connected through the Internet.

Before going into further details, it is important to establish some terminology that will be used throughout the remaining sections and chapters.

- The **Advertiser** is an online server, as explained above, that contains users' public profiles that can be searched and viewed by other users. It gives online accessibility to all its users based on a secured login. It carries only limited information about users (public profiles) based on their level of preferences on exposing personal information that helps improve search results for a potential friend. A user must present his name and email address to register with

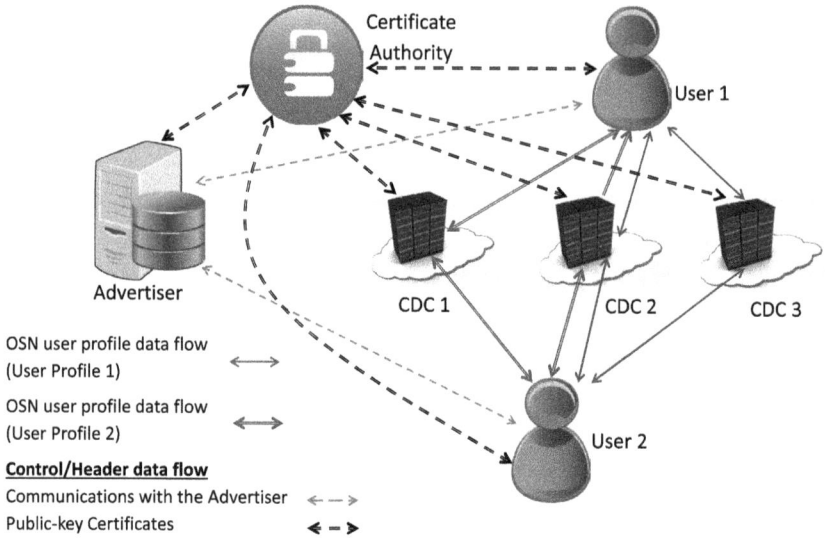

Fig. 3.1   An abstract view of the proposed architecture.

the Advertiser. Other information such as a profile photo, date of birth, current city, education-related information, etc., which can be used as search filters, are optional.

- The **CA** is the trusted certificate authority that certifies ITU-T X.509 based public-key certificates of all the entities in this architecture (users, CDCs, and the Advertiser(s)). In addition to certifying the certificates, it also acts as a repository of public-key certificates and certificate revocation lists (CRLs). These certificates can be used for other information security purposes external to the OSN application as well. Though only a single CA is shown in the figure, the proposed architecture allows for multiple CAs, in which case the CAs have to exchange their public keys securely so that users can verify each other's certificates. However, in this book, only a single CA is considered in the discussion.

- A **user profile** refers to all the information and multimedia data that a user intends to share with his friends. Generally, a user profile in an OSN environment is characterized by a tree hierarchy where the home page is at the root of the tree. Starting from the home page, an authorized user can traverse through the edges to

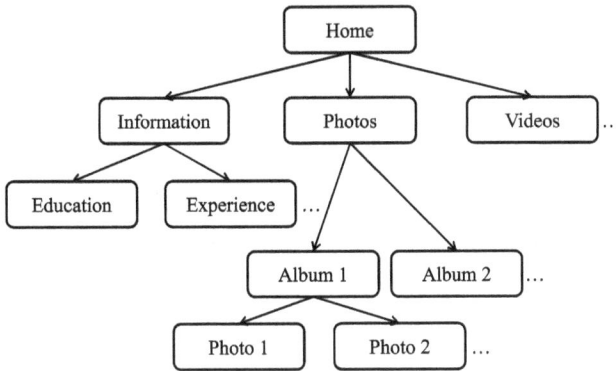

Fig. 3.2 A sample tree hierarchy for a user profile.

the nodes of interest. An example tree structure of a profile is given in Figure 3.2.

- A **profile data page** is any data page that is a node in the tree structure of the user profile.
- The **public profile** has the information (e.g. name, profile picture, etc.) that a user intends to share publicly (e.g. in the Advertiser).
- A **user** refers to the owner of a particular user profile, while a **friend** refers to another user who is authorized by the user to access the user's profile.
- The **Access Computer** is the computing device a user will be using to access the OSN.
- The client application is termed as the **OSN Application**.

3.2 Communications Between Users and CDCs and Advertisers

The communications between a user/friend and a CDC can be broadly categorized into three types. It is important to note that all these communications are initiated only by the user (OSN application).

1. Upload of shares to CDCs.
2. Download of shares from CDCs.
3. Exchange of control messages.

The communications between a user and the Advertiser mainly consist of:

1. communications related to adding, modifying, and deleting public profiles of users resident in the Advertiser,
2. communications related to search queries of friends, and
3. communications that occur when adding a new friend via the Advertiser (The communications involved in adding a friend are explained in detail in Section 4.1.5).

Again, all the above-mentioned communications between the Advertiser and a user and between CDCs and a user are only initiated by the OSN application.

The proposed OSN uses the Secure Hyper Text Transfer Protocol (HTTPS) over TCP/IP [13] to exchange instances of the above mentioned communications. HTTPS sessions are created by OSN applications for each communication they initiate to a CDC or to the Advertiser for processing, and are terminated once a response is received or a timeout occurs. It is the responsibility of the OSN application to initiate an HTTPS session with a CDC or with the Advertiser, and to maintain this session until a response is received. As mentioned above, the CDCs and the Advertiser have no capacity to initiate connections with the OSN application. The OSN application, all the CDCs and the Advertiser must support TLS (Transport Layer Security) version 1.0 [47] or later in order to establish such authenticated sessions.

The public keys required for the SSL/TLS (Secure Socket Layer/Transport Layer Security) sessions are provided in the form of X.509 certificates. All such certificates and CRLs for this OSN architecture are certified by and stored in the trusted CA as shown in Figure 3.1. It is assumed that the URL and the public-key certificate of the CA are known and preconfigured in advance by the user in the OSN application. The CA maintains a directory/database with an {Identifier, public-key certificate} entry for each participant. The set of all the participants in the CA, denoted by P, are $P = A \cup C \cup U$, where A is the set of Advertiser(s), C is the set of all the CDCs, and

U is the set of all the users in the proposed OSN. The "Identifier" needs to be unique for each participant within P. The email address is a good candidate as an identifier for participants in the set U.

3.3 Services and Infrastructure at CDCs

Every CDC provides a virtual private server (VPS) service to each and every user who is registered with the CDC. Such a VPS needs to provide a database service. Hence, the service provided by a CDC in the OSN is of the type PaaS, as explained in Section 1.2. The DB service provided to each user by the CDC in the form of a VPS stores shares of the user profile as different relations (e.g. a relation for user information, a relation for photo albums shared by the user, etc.). Different VPSs are differentiated by unique user identifiers, where user provided email addresses are a good candidate for such an identifier.

In a CDC, there exists a logical entity named the gatekeeper (GK). It provides the following shared services to all the user VPSs:

- Acting as the front end to create SSL sessions when initiated by an OSN application.
- Translating HTTP messages sent by OSN applications to DB queries to be forwarded to DBs in VPSs, and vice versa when replying back to OSN applications.
- Providing first level of access control and authentication. It verifies whether a particular user/friend is authorized to access the targeted VPS by referring to the access control DB which is another service shared by all the users. A user can modify the access control DB entries relevant to the user by requesting the same through the GK. Authentication of users is achieved by unique authentication codes. More information regarding user authentication codes is given in Chapters 4 and 5. User authentication codes are converted into hash values using a secure hash function (e.g. SHA-512) as one-way passwords by the GK before being stored in the access control DB.

A TLS/SSL session is established with the rth CDC's (CDC$_r$) GK using a URL like the following:

https://IP$_{\text{CDC}_r}$/GK:443

Here IP$_{\text{CDC}_r}$ is the user accessible IP address provided by the CDC and GK represents the web application front end of the gatekeeper.

Figure 3.3 provides an architectural block diagram of a CDC (CDC$_r$) with the above-mentioned services. Shown in Figure 3.3 are a user (User i) and one of his friends (Friend j) accessing the VPS service provided to that user by the CDC. All the communications related to these accesses are shown in solid two-way arrows, while the dotted two arrows show communications of the GK with other VPSs. It is important to note that Friend j might or might not be subscribed to the services from CDC$_r$.

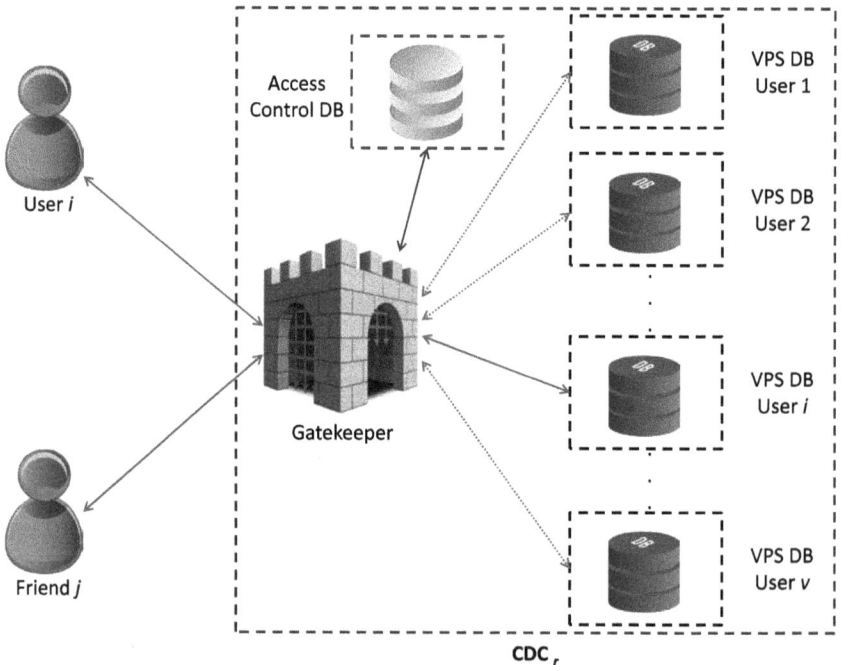

Fig. 3.3 An architectural block diagram of a CDC.

3.4   Summary

The main threat for privacy in conventional OSNs comes from the centralized storage of user data beyond the full control of users. Therefore, we proposed a novel decentralized architecture for online social networking that uses SSS for multimedia data encryption with commercial grade CDCs. This chapter presented the basic network architecture for the proposed OSN, explaining its basic system components: the Advertiser, the CA, the Access Computer, OSN application, CDCs, and allocated VPSs for users. Some terminology was established that will be used in the rest of this book (e.g. a user profile, the public profile, a user, a friend). Services provided at CDCs along with the major components of a CDC's infrastructure, i.e. the gatekeeper, the access control DB, and user VPSs, are also explained with their services for the proposed OSN.

Chapter 4

Operations and Functions in the Proposed OSN

A more robust secure architecture was the prime objective of the proposed OSN. However, it must still have the many functionalities that users tend to expect from an OSN if it is to be accepted and used. This chapter first lists the primary operations and secondary functionalities as a framework to be considered in the proposed OSN. Section 4.1 explains how the proposed architecture can achieve the basic operations expected from an OSN. Then, in Section 4.2, we discuss how the proposed architecture along with secure mechanisms as explained in Chapter 3 can deliver a range of secondary functionalities in an OSN environment, while preserving user privacy.

Richter and Koch in [4] have suggested a list of six basic functionalities in an OSN. Extending this list by adding more functionalities and categorizing them into primary operations and secondary functionalities, we developed the following two lists as a framework to be considered in the proposed OSN. **Primary operations** in an OSN consists of the following:

1. User registration;
2. Creating user profile;
3. Accessing and updating a user profile;
4. Deleting a user profile;
5. Adding friends and contacts to the network;

6. Removing friends and contacts from the network;
7. Accessing friends' profiles.

Similarly, **secondary functionalities** in an OSN are as follows:

1. Searching for contacts according to different criteria;
2. Messaging;
3. Sharing information and content;
4. Wall posting;
5. Commenting on shared content.

The above-mentioned primary operations and secondary functionalities are explained in detail next, along with how they are achieved in the proposed architecture for online social networking.

4.1   Primary Operations in the Proposed OSN

4.1.1   *User registration*

User registration is the very first step for a user in an OSN. Here, it involves two main requirements:

- Registering with n number of CDCs that provide the service requirement for the OSN as explained in Chapter 3. Here n is user defined and $n \geq k$.
- Getting the OSN Application installed in the Access Computer.

4.1.1.1   *Registering with a CDC*

This is the step where a user selects a CDC for the services in the OSN and negotiates terms and parameters of the service. Though it is mentioned as a separate step before the step of installation of the OSN application, the OSN application needs to be in place to create strong authentication codes to be used with the CDCs that the user is going to register with. During this step, the following parameters are exchanged between the user and the CDC:

1. The user provides his email address (that acts as the universal identifier for the user in the OSN) and a user defined/created

authentication code that the user will be using when accessing this particular CDC.

2. The CDC provides the user with the entry {CDC ID, Access IP Address} to be used in the OSN application.

Once both parties agree on the terms of service and exchange the above-mentioned information, the CDC creates a VPS for the user having the email address of the user as the VPS name. Then the CDC administration creates the required DB with all necessary relations, in the allocated VPS of the user with the same name as the VPS. Figure 4.1 shows the schema diagram of the relational database schema of a user profile DB in a CDC with the relevant referential integrity constraints. This schema diagram is just a representative one, particularly the relation "USER_INFO". It may include many other fields such as gender, relationship status, etc.

The CDC also populates the relation USERS in the access control DB with an entry for the new user. The schema diagram for the access control DB is shown in Figure 4.2. Here, the two relations USERS and VISITORS are used for registered users of the CDC and the friends of users (including a self-directed entry for users) authorized to visit the CDC, respectively. SHA-512 is used as the hash algorithm for creating the hash values of the authentication codes in both relations.

4.1.1.2 *Installing the OSN application*

In this phase, the user installs the OSN application in the Access Computer and completes all the necessary configurations. This involves the following steps:

- Accepts a username (e.g. email address) and a password from the user as an access control mechanism to the OSN application.
- Creates a local table/DB (LOCAL_DB) to store CDC-related information and the user has to input that information for all the n number of CDCs to populate the LOCAL_DB. This essentially contains a minimum of four fields: {User_ID, CDC_ID, Access_IP,

USER_INFO

F_Name	M_Name	L_Name	DoB	Email	City	Country	Profile_Pic	Last_Msg_Query

FRIENDS

F_ID	Email	F_Name	M_Name	L_Name	Hash_Auth_Code

EDUCATION

Institute	Qualification	Start	Finish

WORK

Organization	Designation	Start	Finish

ALBUMS

Albm_ID	Name	Thumbnail

PHOTOS

Photo_ID	Albm_ID	Caption	Thumbnail	Photo

PHOTO_COMMENTS

F_ID	Comment_ID	Time_Stamp	Albm_ID	Photo_ID	Accepted	Comment

VIDEOS

Video_ID	Caption	Thumbnail	Video_Path

VIDEO_COMMENTS

F_ID	Comment_ID	Time_Stamp	Video_ID	Accepted	Comment

MSGS

From_F_ID	To_F_ID	Msg_ID	Time_Stamp	Msg

WALL_POSTS

F_ID	Post_ID	Time_Stamp	Accepted	W_Post

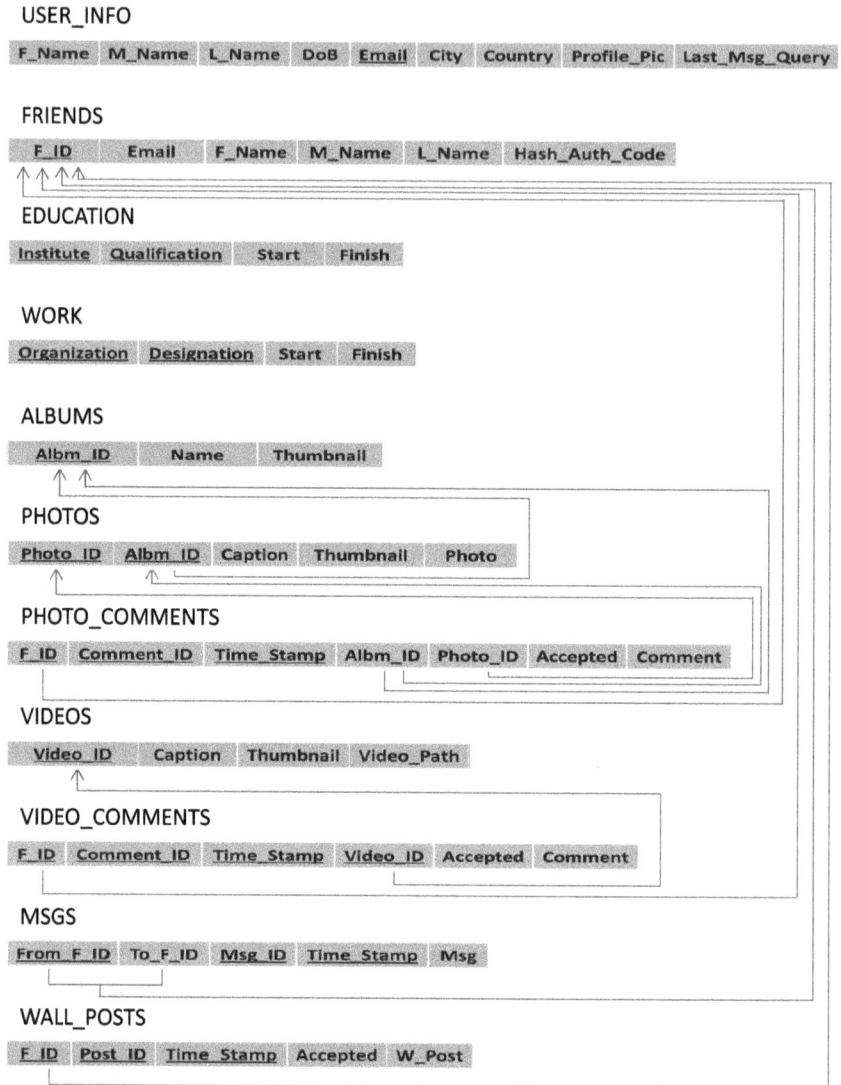

Fig. 4.1 Schema diagram for a user profile relational database schema in a CDC with relevant referential integrity constraints.

Authentication_Code}. In the beginning, this table only has information about the CDCs that the user is registered with. Later on, it facilitates the storage of information about friends' CDCs as well. Here, the User_ID can be the email address as it needs to be

USERS

User_ID	Hash_Auth_Code

VISITORS

Frnd_ID	User_ID	Hash_Auth_Code

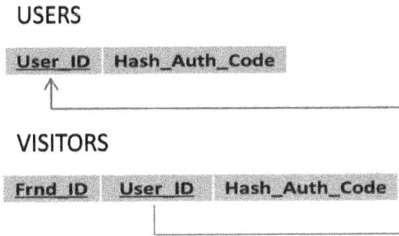

Fig. 4.2 Schema diagram for the access control DB relational database schema in a CDC.

unique for every user. The authentication code is the one that the user provided to the CDC when registering with it.

- Creates a public key, private key pair to be used for all the secure communications as explained in Chapter 3.
- The user registers the entry {identifier, public key} with the CA and the CA creates and certifies the X.509 certificate. The CA also adds the new certificate along with the entry {identifier, public key} to the repository of certificates. The CA also provides the user with its public key that needs to be configured in the OSN application.

The completion of the above-mentioned steps concludes the actions required with the OSN application installation and also the basic operation of "User Registration".

4.1.2 Creating user profile

A user's profile includes a wide range of information to be stored as text, images, and video. As explained in Section 4.1.1, the CDCs have already created a DB with standard relations to capture the whole user profile. The user can use the Graphical User Interface (GUI) features provided by the OSN application to input user profile data. The OSN application creates n number of shares of each profile data item before uploading them to CDCs. The request to upload and store a share in a CDC is transmitted as an HTTP POST request [35] over a secure SSL/TLS session. The general structure of the body of

Source User ID	Target User ID	Auth Code	Upload or Download Request/Control Message

Fig. 4.3   General structure of the body of an HTTP POST request.

an HTTP POST request is shown in Figure 4.3 (the HTTP header is not shown).

Algorithm 1 describes how the GK reacts to such a request. The notation $h(.)$ represents the hash algorithm (e.g. SHA-512) used by the CDC to store hash values of authentication codes. First, it verifies that the user is an authenticated user after checking for an entry in the access control DB. The GK also verifies whether the user is authorized for the upload or download request. If the user is authenticated and authorized, the upload or download requests are forwarded as DB commands/queries to the relevant VPS and the DB. The control messages are further analyzed to check whether the communicating party is the user (owner) of the VPS and the DB, because control messages are special requests from the user to the CDC such as querying for messages, wall posts, etc., that only the users are allowed to make.

As an example, a user with the User ID "S.Crosby@bmail.com" wants to create his profile for the first time. He wishes to upload his first name, last name, country of residence, and profile picture. First the OSN application creates shares of the input that the user has provided. Let those shares be $\{\text{fName}_{sh_1}, \text{lName}_{sh_1}, \text{country}_{sh_1}, \text{profilePic}_{sh_1}\}$, $\{\text{fName}_{sh_2}, \text{lName}_{sh_2}, \text{country}_{sh_2}, \text{profilePic}_{sh_2}\}, \ldots, \{\text{fName}_{sh_r}, \text{lName}_{sh_r}, \text{country}_{sh_r}, \text{profilePic}_{sh_r}\}, \ldots, \{\text{fName}_{sh_n}, \text{lName}_{sh_n}, \text{country}_{sh_n}, \text{profilePic}_{sh_n}\}$. The OSN application then initiates an HTTPS session and sends the HTTP POST request having the fields $\langle$S.Crosby@bmail.com $\|$ S.Crosby@bmail.com $\|$ Authentication Code $\|$ Upload Request$\rangle$ to all n number of CDCs. Assuming the "Authentication Code" is valid, the GK converts the HTTP POST request message to an insert command and forwards it to the VPS and DB named "S.Crosby@bmail.com". The corresponding SQL commands forwarded by the GK of CDC_r would be as follows:

INSERT INTO USER_INFO (F_Name, L_Name, Email, Country, Profile_Pic, Last_Msg_Query)

Algorithm 1: How the GK reacts to an HTTP request.

Data: Source User ID, Target User ID, Auth Code

Result: GK's reaction to an HTTP request

Hash_Auth_Code = h(Auth Code);

num = Number of tuples in relation **VISITORS** in access control DB having the fields {Source User ID, Target User ID, Hash_Auth_Code};

if num== 0 **then**

  | respond "Authentication Failure";

else

  if *message is an upload/download request* **then**

    if *Source User ID is authorized for the requested upload/download* **then**

      | convert the request to a DB command/request and forward to the VPS and the DB named "Target User ID";

    else

      | respond "Unauthorized Request";

    end

  else

    if *Source User ID == Target User ID* **then**

      | act as per the control message request;

    else

      | respond "Unauthorized Request";

    end

  end

end

VALUES (fName$_{shr}$, lName$_{shr}$, 'S. Crosby@bmail.com', country$_{shr}$, profilePic$_{shr}$, 'registration_time');

INSERT INTO FRIENDS(Email, F_Name, L_Name, Hash_Auth_Code)

VALUES ('S.Crosby@bmail.com', fName$_{sh_r}$, lName$_{sh_r}$, $h(auth\_code)$) ;

In the first SQL command, the 'registration_time' is an initialization value for the field "Last_Msg_Query", a field that becomes useful in messaging functionality. The second insert command is required to maintain the referential integrity shown in Figure 4.1 and $h(auth\_code)$ is the hash value of the user's authentication code.

4.1.3   *Accessing and updating a user profile*

Updating a user profile by the user can be any of the following:

- Adding a field value to an empty field.
- Deleting a field value that already exists.
- Modifying an already existing field value with a new one.

Continuing with the above-mentioned example in Section 4.1.2, let us assume the following three scenarios:

(1) The user wants to add a new value to the field "City" in the user profile as "Ottawa". The OSN application creates n number of shares {Ottawa$_{sh_1}$, Ottawa$_{sh_2}$, ..., Ottawa$_{sh_r}$, ..., Ottawa$_{sh_n}$}. Then these shares are forwarded along with the matching upload request message in the message portion of the HTTP POST request message to all the CDCs the user has subscribed to.

(2) The user intends to delete the field entry in the field "Country". The OSN application sends the request to delete the entry as in the above case to all the CDCs.

(3) The user wants to change the profile picture from "profilePic" to "profilePicNew". The OSN creates shares of the file "profilePicNew" as {profilePicNew$_{sh_1}$, profilePicNew$_{sh_2}$, ..., profilePicNew$_{sh_r}$, ..., profilePicNew$_{sh_n}$}. The OSN application sends the matching request to update the field "Profile_Pic" along with a share as in the above cases to all the CDCs.

After receiving the HTTP POST requests from the user and following Algorithm 1, the GKs of all the CDCs convert them to the appropriate DB commands and forward those to the VPS and the DB named "S.Crosby@bmail.com". As an example, the corresponding SQL commands at the CDC_r would be as follows:

For Case 1:

UPDATE USER_INFO
SET City = Ottawa$_{shr}$
WHERE Email = 'S.Crosby@bmail.com';

For Case 2:

UPDATE USER_INFO
SET Country = **NULL**
WHERE Email = 'S.Crosby@bmail.com';

For Case 3:

UPDATE USER_INFO
SET Profile_Pic = profilePicNew$_{shr}$
WHERE Email = 'S.Crosby@bmail.com';

Accessing a user's own profile would simply mean reviewing the user's own profile at a later point in time. In order to do that, the OSN application follows two steps:

(1) Read the LOCAL_DB and select the entries related only to the user as this table contains friends' information as well. Out of the selected n number of entries, choose any k randomly. Read CDC IDs, IP addresses and Authentication codes in each entry that corresponds to each CDC of the ones chosen.
(2) Initiate SSL sessions with the GKs of the selected k number of CDCs and send HTTP POST requests asking for the shares relevant to the profile information the user is interested in.

At the GK of a CDC, upon receiving the above-mentioned request from the user's OSN application and after following Algorithm 1, the GK converts the request to a set of matching SQL queries.

As an example, let us consider the case where the user in the above-mentioned example wants to review his profile homepage. The GK of the CDC_r sends the following SQL query to the VPS (and the DB) allocated to the user.

SELECT F_Name, M_Name, L_Name, DoB, Email, City, Country, Profile_Pic
FROM USER_INFO
WHERE Email = 'S.Crosby@bmail.com';

Upon receiving a response for the above-mentioned query from the DB allocated to the user, the GK translates the response to an HTTP response and sends it over the SSL session to the OSN application of the user. Once the OSN application receives the complete response, it terminates the SSL session. After receiving all the responses from k number of CDCs, the OSN application uses the relevant shares to reconstruct the original secret and then displays the profile information the user was originally interested in, in this case, the user's profile homepage.

4.1.4 *Deleting user profiles*

A user's decision to withdraw from the OSN and delete his profile is achieved in the following two main steps:

1. Delete all profile data shares stored in all CDCs. This means that all the relations corresponding to the user's profile are deleted in the DB allocated to the user in each CDC. For example, such a request is translated into SQL commands by a GK as follows:

   DELETE FROM USER_INFO;
   DELETE FROM FRIENDS;
   DELETE FROM EDUCATION;
   DELETE FROM WORK;
   DELETE FROM ALBUMS;
   DELETE FROM PHOTOS;
   DELETE FROM PHOTO_COMMENTS;

DELETE FROM VIDEOS;
DELETE FROM VIDEO_COMMENTS;
DELETE FROM MESSAGES;
DELETE FROM WALL_POSTS;

2. Delete the public profile hosted at the Advertiser. Just as in the case with CDCs, the OSN application requests that the Advertiser remove the public profile entry at the Advertiser, in the form of an HTTP POST request over an SSL session. The Advertiser front end converts this request to a DB command and forwards it to the Advertiser DB. As an example, considering the same profile as before, such an SQL command would be as follows, where PUBLIC_PROFILES is the name of the relation where the Advertiser keeps public profile records of all the users of the OSN.

DELETE FROM PUBLIC_PROFILES
WHERE User_ID = 'S.Crosby@bmail.com';

Following the above two steps will simply remove a user's subscription from the OSN. However, it is also required to contact the CDCs later to inform them to cease the service they are providing to the user. Once such a notice is received, the CDC administration can reallocate the resources provided to the user back to the pool of resources or to any other purpose.

4.1.5 *Adding friends and contacts to the network*

Once two friends are connected with each other in an OSN, they should be able to view each other's profiles and also be able to carry out interactive functions like wall posting, commenting, and messaging. In the proposed OSN architecture, this would imply that two friends have to share access details of each other's registered CDCs along with matching authentication codes. Users of the OSN can exchange such information in any format. However, in this architecture, we propose to create a header file that carries such information about a single user and exchange that header file with the new friend.

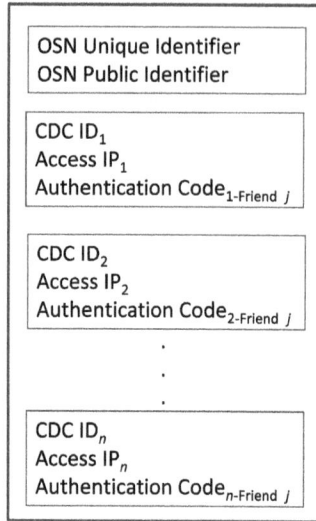

Fig. 4.4   Format of a header file.

The OSN application is capable of both creating such a header file and reading one. Figure 4.4 shows the format of such a header file created for a new friend, Friend j, by the user. Here the OSN unique identifier identifies the user uniquely within the OSN, such as the email address of the user. The OSN public identifier is how the user is known among his friends within the OSN, such as his name or any other alias and this may not be unique within the OSN. After these two identifiers, all the n number of CDCs the user is registered with are listed as entries {CDC ID, Access IP, Authentication Code}. In Figure 4.4, CDC ID_r is the unique ID of CDC_r, Access IP_r is the public IP address provided by CDC_r to the user to be used as the entry point by the user and his friends when accessing the user profile share in that CDC, and Authentication $\text{Code}_{r-\text{Friend } j}$ is the authentication code offered to Friend j to access the user's profile shares in CDC_r. The authentication codes created/offered to all the friends should not be the same. Ideally there should not be a way for an adversary to derive the authentication code assigned to Friend j to acccss the user's CDC_r. Therefore, all the authentication codes are created randomly by the OSN application.

The above-mentioned header files can be exchanged in numerous ways between two new friends as deemed secure by the users, using a secure channel. For example, they can exchange them over emails or they can physically exchange them using portable storage devices. Such secure channels are out-of-band of the OSN. However, to provide flexibility, user friendliness, and swiftness, we propose a mechanism that makes use of resources already available in the OSN architecture. In this method, the Advertiser acts as the arbitrator and the main link between two new friends when they do the first "handshake" of becoming friends, i.e. the exchange of header files and allowing access to the new friend to the user's DBs in CDCs. Figure 4.5 illustrates the handshake protocol when new friends are added through the Advertiser. In Figure 4.5, the friend request initiator is Alice and she wishes to add Bob as her friend. All the communications between the users and the CA, and the users and the Advertiser are done through HTTPS sessions.

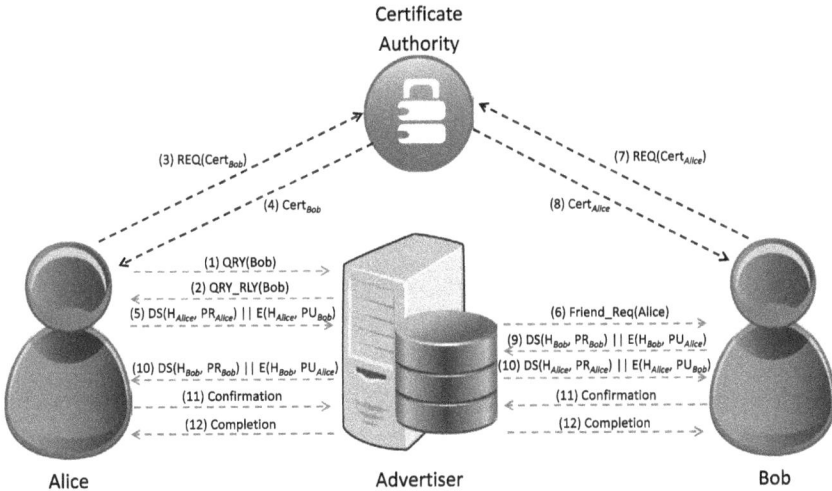

Fig. 4.5 The handshake protocol of adding a friend.

The steps involved in the handshake protocol for adding friends are explained as follows according to Figure 4.5:

1. Alice queries the Advertiser for "Bob" as a search query.
2. The Advertiser replies to Alice's query with all the matching entries with their OSN unique identifiers.
3. Alice picks the correct entry for Bob (if there is more than one matching result from the Advertiser) and decides to add Bob as her friend. Alice (her OSN application) requests the public-key certificate of Bob (Cert_{Bob}) from the CA.
4. The CA replies back to Alice with Cert_{Bob}.
5. Alice encrypts her header file (H_{Alice}) using Bob's public key (PU_{Bob}) with an RSA-based encryption algorithm (e.g. RSAES-OAEP Algorithm [18]). Alice then creates a digital signature to append the encrypted header file using her private key (PR_{Alice}) with an RSA-based digital signature scheme (e.g. RSASSA-PSS Algorithm [18]). Alice sends the digital signature and the encrypted header file i.e. $DS(H_{Alice}, PR_{Alice}) \parallel E(H_{Alice}, PU_{Bob})$, with other message specific parameters to indicate the message's intention (to add Bob as friend) to the Advertiser as an HTTP POST request. Figure 4.6 is a block diagram that shows the steps involved in the creation of the HTTP POST request. The general format of this HTTP POST request is given in Figure 4.7.
6. The Advertiser buffers the friend request from Alice and sends a notification to Bob regarding the pending friend request (when Bob queries the Advertiser for any updates, in the form of a control message, again as an HTTP POST request).
7. Upon receiving the friend request, Bob can either accept or reject it. If Bob rejects it, it gets communicated to the Advertiser and the Advertiser communicates the same to Alice (as a response to a query from Alice), and the process ends there. If Bob decides to accept the friend request, then the protocol continues and he requests Alice's public-key certificate (Cert_{Alice}) from the CA.
8. The CA replies back to Bob with Cert_{Alice}.
9. Just like Alice did, Bob encrypts his header file (H_{Bob}) using Alice's public key (PU_{Alice}) with the same RSA-based

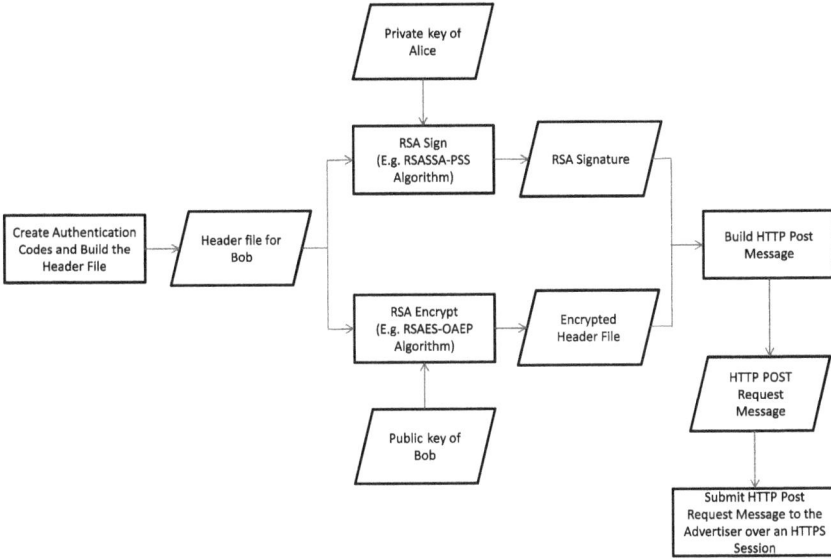

Fig. 4.6 The process diagram of creating the HTTP POST request message to send the user header file to a friend.

encryption algorithm and appends it with the digital signature created using the same RSA-based digital signature scheme and his private key (PR_{Bob}). Bob sends the digital signature and the encrypted header file i.e. $DS(H_{Bob}, PR_{Bob}) \parallel E(H_{Bob}, PU_{Alice})$, with other message-specific parameters to indicate the message's intention (to accept Alice's friend request) to the Advertiser as an HTTP POST request.

10. Upon receiving the acceptance and the message from Bob, the Advertiser forwards the message from Alice to Bob i.e. $DS(H_{Alice}, PR_{Alice}) \parallel E(H_{Alice}, PU_{Bob})$, and the message from Bob to Alice, i.e. $DS(H_{Bob}, PR_{Bob}) \parallel E(H_{Bob}, PU_{Alice})$.

11. Once Alice and Bob receive their messages, they decrypt the encrypted messages using their private keys and verify the digital signature using other party's public key. Upon verification, the information in the header file is used to make entries in the LOCAL_DB for the new friend. Each user must also inform his or her CDCs about the new friend and request that they add the

HTTP Header
Message Specific Parameters (Message Type = Add Friend, Source User ID, Target User ID)
RSA Signature (DS(H$_{Alice}$, PR$_{Alice}$))
Encrypted Header Fie (E(H$_{Alice}$, PU$_{Bob}$))

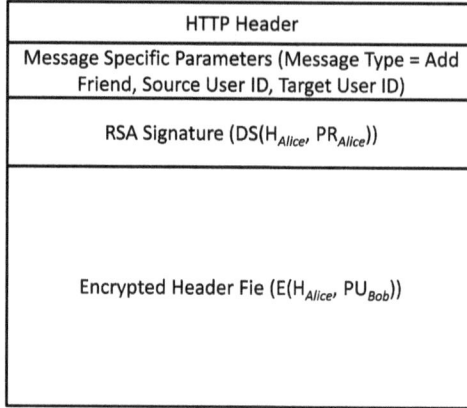

Fig. 4.7   The format of an HTTP POST request to add a friend.

new friend to both the VISITORS relation in the access control DB and to the FRIENDS relation in the user's DB in the VPS allocated to him or her. As an example, the GK, in CDC$_r$ of Alice would convert such a request to an SQL command as follows:

INSERT INTO FRIENDS(Email , F_Name , M_Name , L_Name , Hash_Auth_Code)
VALUES (Email$_{Bob}$, fName$_{Bob-sh_r}$, mName$_{Bob-sh_r}$, lName$_{Bob-sh_r}$, $h(auth\_code_{Bob_r})$) ;

Email$_{Bob}$ is Bob's email address (OSN unique identifier), fName, mName, lName are Bob's first, middle, and last names respectively and $h(auth\_code \ _{Bob_r})$ is the hash value of the authentication code Alice created for Bob to access the CDC$_r$. Figure 4.8 illustrates the process of decrypting and verifying the digital signature at Bob, once he receives the header file from the Advertiser, sent by Alice. Once both Alice and Bob have carried out the above mentioned DB updates, they confirm back to the Advertiser that they have completed the necessary DB updates.

12. The Advertiser communicates to both parties that now they are ready to act as friends and completes the handshake protocol that connected Alice and Bob as friends.

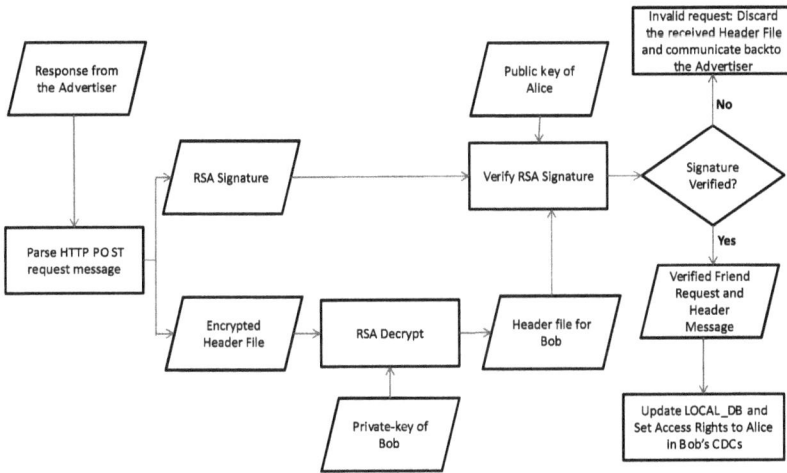

Fig. 4.8 The process diagram of processing of an HTTP response message received to add a friend carrying the friend's header file.

It is important to note that the Advertiser does not initiate any of the communications in the above-mentioned handshake protocol. It merely responds with the available status to users when they send query/request messages.

4.1.6 *Removing friends and contacts from the network*

Removing a friend would logically mean two things:

- The user does not intend to access the friend's profile anymore.
- The user does not want the friend to access his profile.

For the first requirement, the OSN application just has to remove the entries corresponding to the friend in the LOCAL_DB. To block the friend from accessing the user's profile in the future, the OSN application simply has to inform all the n number of CDCs to delete the entry for that friend. The GK consequently issues commands to delete the corresponding entry in the two DBs, access control DB, and the DB maintained in the VPS allocated to keep the user's profile shares. As an example, let us assume that the user in the previous examples has a friend having the user ID "K.Senevirathna@bmail.com" and he wishes to remove this user from his network of friends. The corresponding SQL command by the GK to the access control DB is

DELETE FROM VISITORS
WHERE Frnd_ID = 'K.Senevirathna@bmail.com' **AND**
   User_ID = 'S.Crosby@bmail.com';

The corresponding SQL command by the GK to the user profile DB is

DELETE FROM FRIENDS
WHERE Email = 'K.Senevirathna@bmail.com';

4.1.7   *Accessing friends' profiles*

When accessing a friend's profile, the user simply becomes a "friend" from the friend's point of view. In such a case, the following steps are performed by the OSN application:

1. Access the LOCAL_DB and query all the entries that match the field USER_ID with the friend's ID (email address).
2. Select any k number of entries from the result in the above query and read the entries {CDC_ID, Access_IP, Authentication_Code} for all the k number of CDCs.
3. Contact the trusted CA and download the public key certificates for all the k number of CDCs (if not already available).
4. Using the downloaded public key certificates, initiate SSL/TLS sessions with each GK of CDCs and request the friend's profile shares in the form of HTTP POST requests. The message format is the same as given in Figure 4.3.

GKs at every CDC follow Algorithm 1 before proceeding with the user's request. Upon verifying that the user is eligible to access friend's profile data, a DB query is created and forwarded to the DB that keeps the friend's profile data. The GK responds back to the OSN application of the user with an HTTP response message that carries the response from the DB. Once a response is received, the OSN application terminates the SSL/TLS session with that GK. Upon successfully receiving all the k number of shares of the profile data that the user was interested in, the OSN application reconstructs the original secret values of the friend's profile to be displayed to the user.

4.2 Secondary Functionalities of the OSN

4.2.1 *Searching for contacts according to different criteria*

As explained in Chapter 3, the Advertiser provides an indexing service in the OSN by advertising user public profiles. It provides searching capability to the users of the OSN for potential friends. The searching capability can provide advanced filtering criteria for OSN users based on their name, age, date of birth, high school, college/University, employer, etc. Such filtering gets converted to a DB query at the Advertiser. Theoretically, the proposed architecture can accommodate more than one Advertiser, and they work independently without a need for integration or synchronization.

4.2.2 *Wall posting*

A wall is simply a personal blog for each user where he can post a textual message to be seen by his friends. Friends also can post messages on a user's wall. Generally, all wall posts of a user are visible to all of his friends. In conventional OSNs, friends can post on a user's wall without the consent of the user. However, in the proposed OSN, a wall post from a friend requires the user's approval before being posted on the wall. As an example, let us assume that a friend with the email address F_j_email wants to post a message on user's wall. Once the friend inputs the wall post, his OSN application acts as follows:

1. The OSN application accesses the LOCAL_DB and selects the n number of entries carrying CDC information for the user, finds the value of n, as this can be different from user to user, and reads the values CDC_ID, Access_IP, and Authentication_Code for all the n number of entries.
2. The OSN application then creates n number of shares using (k, n) threshold secret sharing for text.
3. Next, it creates a Post_ID (can be a random numeric ID) that represents the wall post. This Post_ID will be the same for all the shares of the same wall post.
4. Finally, it initiates SSL/TLS sessions with all the n number of CDCs of the user, and sends HTTP POST requests to upload the shares. The Post_ID created for the wall post and a time stamp (based on GMT-Greenwich Mean Time) is attached to the HTTP POST request and will be the same for all shares of the wall post sent to n number of CDCs.

The GKs at all CDCs authenticate the friend before creating and forwarding the DB command. Assuming that the GK at CDC_r received a request to post a wall message with a post ID *222567* and a time stamp '2014-05-24 09:12:47.430' carrying the rth share of the secret wall post, i.e. $wall\_post_{sh_r}$, it first queries for the "F_ID" value of the friend with the SQL query;

SELECT F_ID
FROM FRIENDS
WHERE Email = 'F_j_email';

Let the result of the above query be F_ID_j. Then the GK at CDC_r issues the following SQL command to the user DB in the VPS to store the wall post sent by the friend.

INSERT INTO WALL_POSTS (F_ID, Post_ID, Time_Stamp, Accepted, W_Post)
VALUES (F_ID$_j$, 222567, '2014−05−24 09:12:47.430', 0, $wall\_post_{sh_r}$);

The value for the field "Accepted" in the inserted entry is initialized with the value '0' to indicate the fact that the wall post is yet to be approved by the user. Only the tuples with the value '1', which indicates user approval, are displayed when an OSN application queries for wall posts of a particular user.

A user OSN application makes use of a set of control messages/ queries apart from the upload and download requests for certain control purposes, as shown in Figure 4.3. Such control messages are discussed when their use is explained in the context of an OSN function. They are communicated in the form of HTTP POST requests in the following instances:

1. When a user logs into the OSN application.
2. Periodically while the user is logged into the OSN application (the time intervals in such periodic control messages and queries are design parameters).
3. Whenever a requirement arises for a control message due to user activities in the OSN.

In the context of wall posts, a user queries all the CDCs whenever a user logs into the OSN application as well as periodically while he is logged in, for wall posts that are pending for user approval. The GK of a CDC converts such a query from the user OSN application to the following SQL query and forwards it to the user DB in the VPS.

SELECT *
FROM WALL_POSTS
WHERE Accepted = 0;

The response from the DB is forwarded by the GK to the user OSN application. The GUI of the user OSN application shows the user how many wall posts are pending and what they are. The user may approve or discard such wall posts at his discretion. The reconstruction of wall posts is done with k number of shares of the same wall post. The OSN application differentiates between different wall posts based on the fields "Email", "Post_ID", and "Time_Stamp" because these three fields are the same for every share of a single wall post (created by a particular friend's or the user's OSN application) and are unique from other wall posts. Also, the "Time_Stamp" field allows the OSN application to display the wall posts in chronological order. The requirement for wall post reconstruction is due to two reasons:

- Approved wall posts are reconstructed to be viewed by the user and/or his friends at any given point of time, as desired by the user and his friends.
- Pending wall posts need to be reconstructed to be reviewed by the user for his approval.

If the user decides to discard a wall post, the OSN application informs this intention to all the n number of CDCs in the form of a control message. The GK converts this to an SQL command and forwards it to the user DB in the VPS. For example, if the user decided to discard the wall post discussed in the previous example, the SQL command from all the GKs of the n number of CDCs to the user DBs in the VPSs is as follows:

DELETE FROM WALL_POSTS
WHERE F_ID = F_ID$_j$ **AND** Post_ID = 222567 **AND**
    Time_Stamp = '2014−05−24 09:12:47.430 ';

When the user or a friend wants to view all of a user's wall posts, the OSN application requests shares of all wall posts from k number of the user's CDCs. Such a request is transformed into an SQL query by a GK as follows:

SELECT Email , F_Name, M_Name, L_Name, Post_ID ,
    Time_Stamp , W_Post
FROM WALL_POSTS, FRIENDS
WHERE Accepted=1 **AND** WALL_POSTS.F_ID=FRIENDS.F_ID
ORDER BY Time_Stamp ;

The response carries shares of the wall post author's name, the ID of the post, the time stamp and shares of the wall post itself. Using these shares and information, an OSN application can reconstruct the original wall post and its author's name and display all the wall posts chronologically along with their authors' names.

4.2.3 *Messaging*

Messages are discrete textual communications between a user and a friend. Storing message shares is somewhat similar to storing shares of wall posts as presented in Section 4.2.2. However, there exist certain differences listed as follows:

- Messages do not require user approval.
- Messages need to be displayed to the user once queried after being grouped under different friends and only the ones queried, i.e. when the communication history between the user and a particular friend is queried, only the messages between these two entities should get displayed.
- Shares of the same message need to be stored in both the user's DBs in all his CDCs as well as the friend's DBs in his CDCs.
- Friends are not allowed the READ access to the message history storage of the user at all, since the message history between the friend and the user is stored in the friend's DBs in CDCs as well.

The number of shares of a message created depends on the secret sharing threshold scheme used by the user and the friend. A friend's threshold scheme can always be found by referring to the LOCAL_DB and counting the number of entries under that friend's ID. Let us assume that the user has a threshold secret-sharing scheme of (k, n) and the friend has a threshold scheme of (k, m). As mentioned in Chapter 3, k is a design parameter and is therefore already known. If N is the number of shares required to be created, then

$$N = \max(m, n) \tag{4.1}$$

As an example, let us consider a scenario where the user intends to send a message to one of his friends and we assume the following parameters:

- User's ID: "S.Crosby@bmail.com"
- Friend's ID: "K.Senevirathna@bmail.com"
- User's threshold secret-sharing scheme: (k, n)
- Friend's threshold secret-sharing scheme: (k, m)
- Message ID: 178954
- Time stamp: "2014-05-24 10:15:12.892"
- F_ID of K.Senevirathna@bmail.com in user's DBs in VPSs in CDCs: 215
- F_ID of S.Crosby@bmail.com in friend's DBs in VPSs in CDCs: 547.

Let the message be 'M' and the shares of it created by the OSN application of the user be $\{M_{sh_1}, M_{sh_2}, \ldots, M_{sh_r}, \ldots, M_{sh_t}, \ldots, M_{sh_N}\}$. Here $r, t \leq m, n$ and N is selected according to Equation (4.1).

The user's OSN application sends n number of shares of the message 'M' to all the n number of CDCs the user has subscribed to. Upon authentication, the GK of CDC_r forwards the following SQL command to the DB named "S.Crosby@bmail.com" in the VPS carrying the same identifier name.

INSERT INTO MSGS(From_F_ID , To_F_ID , MSG_ID ,
    Time_Stamp , Msg)
VALUES (0 , 215 , 178954 , '2014−05−24
    10:15:12.892 ' , M_{sh_r});

Simultaneously, the user's OSN application sends m number of shares of the message 'M' to all the m number of CDCs the friend has subscribed to. Upon authentication, the GK of tth CDC of the friend (CDC_t) forwards the following SQL command to the DB named 'K.Senevirathna@bmail.com' in the VPS having the same identifier name.

INSERT INTO MSGS(From_F_ID , To_F_ID , MSG_ID ,
   Time_Stamp , Msg)
VALUES (547 , 0 , 178954 , '2014−05−24
   10:15:12.892 ' , M_{sh_t});

The user needs to get notifications of new messages from friends. As explained in Section 4.2.2, control messages are used by an OSN application to query new messages from all the users. The GK makes use of the field "Last_Msg_Query" in the relation "USER_INFO" for this purpose. Let T_{last} be the time stamp stored in the field "Last_Msg_Query", and let the current time be $T_{current}$. Upon receiving a control message querying for unread messages from a user's OSN application, the GK queries the user's DB in the VPS all messages (excluding the ones uploaded by the user himself) that satisfy the requirement $Time\_Stamp > T_{last}$, and then set the field "Last_Msg_Query" to $T_{current}$. As an example, the corresponding SQL query and the command are as follows:

SELECT FRIENDS.Email , **COUNT**($*$)
FROM MSGS, USER_INFO , FRIENDS
WHERE Time_Stamp>LAST_MSG_QUERY **AND** FROM_F_ID>0
   AND FROM_F_ID=F_ID
GROUP BY FRIENDS.Email ;

UPDATE USER_INFO
SET Last_Msg_Query = $T_{current}$
WHERE Email='S.Crosby@bmail.com ';

The given SQL query returns to the GK how many different new messages the DB has received and stored after $time = T_{last}$, grouping the results under email addresses of friends. The GK forwards the same to the user's OSN application, which shows a notification to the user, the number of new messages the user has received, and the names of the friends who sent them (after referring to the LOCAL_DB). If the user has not checked the last notification, the OSN application simply adds the new message count to the previous results and updates the notification.

The time interval between two queries for new messages, from the OSN application to the CDCs while the user is logged in is an important design parameter. The shorter the time interval, the more the experience for the user will be more real-time. However, shortening the time interval will result in communication overhead in the network and processing overhead at the user-allocated VPS and the GK of a CDC.

Reviewing messages is subtly different from reviewing wall posts as only the messages sent by the user to a particular friend and vice versa should be displayed to the user. As an example, when reviewing the message history of the user and a friend (e.g. the friend with the email address "K.Senevirathna@bmail.com"), a GK has to send the following SQL query to the user DB in the VPS, and respond back to the user OSN application with the query response. The response received is ordered by the time stamp, hence the messages are in chronological order.

SELECT F_Name, M_Name, L_Name, Email, Msg_ID,
    Time_Stamp, Msg
FROM MSGS, FRIENDS
WHERE (To_F_ID **IN** (**SELECT** F_ID **FROM** FRIENDS
    WHERE Email='K.Senevirathna@bmail.com') **OR**
    From_F_ID **IN** (**SELECT** F_ID **FROM** FRIENDS
    WHERE Email='K.Senevirathna@bmail.com'))
    AND F_ID=From_F_ID
ORDER BY Time_Stamp;

4.2.4   *Sharing information and content*

As discussed in Chapter 3, users of an OSN expect to share content and information with their friends through the OSN. Information shared in an OSN is textual and shared content can be text, image, or video. As explained in Chapter 3, whatever the content type is, secret sharing can be used to create shares of that content. Once the shares are created, they need to be uploaded to the DBs in VPSs of all CDCs of a user. Content is shared by friends of a user as well as by the user himself. However, the content shared by a friend is in the form of wall posts, messages and comments on shared content, which are covered in detail in Sections 4.2.2, 4.2.3, and 4.2.5 respectively.

In this section, we will focus on content shared by the user himself. Sharing of textual content is the same as explained in Sections 4.1.2 and 4.1.3, where the GK of a CDC issues "INSERT" or "UPDATE" DB commands as needed to store the shares of the secret textual data (e.g. user's profile information, wall posts, etc.) along with its relevant metadata. When sharing photos, it is expected of the user to create an album to put the photos in. As shown in Figure 4.1, an album may contain a name given by the user as well as a thumbnail, which is a scaled-down version of a photo the user selects. The "Album_ID" is the primary key in the relation created for albums and it is an auto-increment field. In the relation "PHOTOS", there exists a referential integrity constraint "Album_ID" that refers to the primary key in the relation "ALBUMS" with the same field name. When uploading photos, a thumbnail is also created for each photo. The GUI of the OSN application shows thumbnails of all the photos first. Then once the user picks a photo from the set of thumbnails, the original photo is displayed by the OSN application. It is important to note that all the photos and thumbnails stored in CDCs are just shares created using image secret sharing.

As an example, let us assume the user with the email address "S.Crosby@bmail.com" wants to create a new photo album named "Summer 2013". After specifying the album name, the user selects the images to be uploaded to the album with an image to be used as the thumbnail of the album. The OSN application creates n number of shares of all the photos and thumbnails. Let the user upload one image 'I' where the thumbnail of the same is the thumbnail of the album. Let the shares of the image be $\{I_{sh_1}, I_{sh_2}, \ldots, I_{sh_r}, \ldots, I_{sh_n}\}$ and the shares of the thumbnail be $\{TN_{sh_1}, TN_{sh_2}, \ldots, TN_{sh_r}, \ldots, TN_{sh_n}\}$. The GK of CDC_r forwards the following SQL command to the DB in the VPS named "S.Crosby@bmail.com", after verifying the user's authenticity.

INSERT INTO ALBUMS(Name, Thumbnail)
VALUES ('Summer 2013', TN_{sh_r});

INSERT INTO PHOTOS(Album_ID, Caption, Thumbnail, Photo)
VALUES ($abmid$, caption$_{sh_r}$, TN_{sh_r}, I_{sh_r});

Here '$abmid$' is the auto-incremented Album_ID of the album "Summer 2013" and 'caption$_{sh_r}$' is the share of the textual caption user attached to the posted image.

Video posting follows almost the same process as photo posting except for the following differences:

- There is not a relation similar to "ALBUMS" that is related to video posts. The OSN application takes the first frame of the video as the image for the thumbnail.
- In the relation "VIDEOS", only the path for the video share file is recorded, rather than the video share itself. The video share is stored in a directory in the same VPS that is allocated to the user in a CDC, of which the location is given by the "Video_Path" field in the "VIDEOS" relation.

4.2.5   *Commenting on shared content*

Comments have the same characteristics as wall posts. The only difference is that the comments are posted in the context of shared content such as a photo or a video. As in wall posts, comments do need user approval before being posted. This architecture provides two relations to store comments for photos and videos separately. Posting comments, querying for comments that are waiting for user approval in the form of a control message, approving comments by the user, and reviewing comments follow the same processes as for wall posts, which are described in detail in Section 4.2.2. Comments are always displayed along with relevant shared content. As an example, when the image 'I' in the previous example is requested to be viewed by an OSN application from the CDC_r, the GK sends the following SQL queries (assuming 'I' is the first photo in its album) to the user DB in the allocated VPS, before responding back to the OSN application with the requested information.

SELECT Caption , Photo
FROM PHOTOS
WHERE Photo_ID = 1 **AND** Album_ID = *abmid*;

SELECT F_Name, M_Name, L_Name, Comment_ID ,
    Time_Stamp , Photo_ID , Album_ID , Comment
FROM PHOTO_COMMENTS , FRIENDS
WHERE Photo_ID = 1 **AND** Album_ID = *abmid* **AND**
    Accepted = 1 **AND** PHOTO_COMMENTS . F_ID =
    FRIENDS . F_ID
ORDER BY Time_Stamp ;

Once k number of shares of the image and comments are received, the OSN application sorts shares of comments based on "F_ID", "Comment_ID", and "Time_Stamp", and reconstructs comments using k number of shares that carry the same values for these three fields. Once all the comments are reconstructed along with their authors' names, they are displayed in chronological order with authors' names.

4.2.6 *Other functions*

There are certain secondary functionalities that are present in today's OSNs that we did not consider in this architecture. Identity management that involves setting access rights in a higher granularity to friends for different shared content by the user, and tagging people in shared multimedia content were two such functionalities that were outside of the scope of this study, and could be future research directions. Also, predicting and informing contacts proactively by the OSN, context awareness (shows how a particular user is connected to another user), and news feeds and notifications to provide awareness of users' activities in the OSN are some secondary functionalities that we ignored in the proposed architecture due to potential violation of privacy associated with those functionalities.

4.3 Summary

The proposed architecture considers user registration, creating a user profile, accessing and updating a user profile, deleting a user profile, adding contacts to the user's network of friends, removing friends from the network, and accessing friends' profiles as primary operations in an OSN environment. It also provides support for the secondary functionalities of searching for contacts, wall posting, messaging, sharing information and content, and commenting on shared content. How these primary operations and secondary functionalities are realized in the proposed OSN is discussed in greater detail in this chapter. User authentication and access control at GKs is implemented as per Algorithm 1. A representative relational database schema of a user profile DB in a VPS that resides in a CDC was presented, and it was used as a reference in the discussion of implementation of primary operations and secondary functionalities. This chapter also discussed the different message types and their formats in the proposed OSN along with the secure handshake protocol to be used when adding new contacts to the friend network of a user via the Advertiser.

Part III

Prototype Implementation and Analysis of SecureCSocial

Chapter 5

Security Analysis of the Proposed Architecture

As mentioned in Chapter 1, the primary objective of this study is to propose an architecture for online social networking with a trust model that only trusts a users' friends but none else, while ensuring that it still provides the functionalities available in most conventional OSNs. Therefore, security and privacy is one of the most crucial design considerations in the proposed OSN. In this chapter, we analyze the proposed architecture for its security or vulnerability from several perspectives, starting with the justification for why SSS was chosen as the method of data encryption prior to storage, in Section 5.1. Section 5.2 analyzes the proposed OSN for its vulnerability against different potential adversaries, i.e. other nonfriend OSN users, the Advertiser(s), CDCs, the CA, and other entities external to the OSN. Different primary operations and secondary functionalities of the proposed OSN are analyzed for security as per the security services defined in the X.800 standard as applicable, in Section 5.3. Section 5.4 analyzes the resiliency of the proposed OSN architecture against the range of attacks presented in [21]. Finally, CDCs being a major system component in the proposed architecture, Section 5.5 discusses the capability of the proposed OSN to withstand known security risks in cloud computing.

5.1 Why SSS?

While there are many encryption algorithms available today for encrypting data before confidentially storing them, we chose SSS to encrypt and create shares of users' profile data to be stored in CDCs, due to the following reasons:

- SSS is considered to be an **information theoretically secure** cryptographic algorithm [16]. In other words, incorporating secret sharing into the proposed OSN provides a platform for higher information security than other encryption algorithms can provide.
- One of the important benefits of using secret sharing is the flexibility it provides to support the **dynamic nature of social networks** in the online domain, especially when removing a friend from a user's network. In such a situation, storing profile data using a key-based algorithm such as DES or AES would require replacing encrypted data with new data, encrypted using a new key. Otherwise, an "ex-friend" collaborating with the data storage provider (or a malicious insider of the data storage provider) would compromise a user's profile and all his future activities. To make things even more challenging, the user would have to redistribute the new key to his existing friends, with a notice of change. In the proposed OSN, simply notifying all of the user's CDCs to block the friend (remove all access rights) would be sufficient to effectively remove that friend.
- Storing shares of profile data in n number of CDCs, where $n > k$ provides **high availability**. For example, a failure of the system of the storage provider in traditional key-based encryption data storage, due to reasons such as technical failures and Denial-of-Service (DoS) attacks, would make a user's profile inaccessible to the user and all of his friends. In other words, such a system inherits a single-point-of-failure. In SSS, all that is required to create the original secret is k number of shares. Thus, the proposed architecture is more robust against a failure of a user's CDC, as long as $n > k$.

- The **level of risk of a user's profile being exposed to a CDC (or a malicious employee working for a CDC) is greatly reduced** by using secret sharing in the proposed OSN. In traditional encryption algorithms, from the data storage provider's perspective, all it takes to compromise a user's profile is the encryption key(s). As mentioned above, there can be numerous ways for an adversary to obtain the encryption key(s) in an OSN environment, thus making a user's profile more vulnerable. However, in secret sharing, such a risk is reduced to a great extent as the security of the algorithm does not depend on a secret key, but on k number of shares, to which getting access is more challenging for an adversary.

Having provided the justification for using SSS in the proposed architecture, next we will analyze its vulnerability from the perspective of different threat agents present in the system.

5.2 Protecting User Privacy from Different Potential Adversaries

In this section, we analyze the proposed architecture for its strength and vulnerability against different potential threat agents. Different entities to be considered in such an analysis can be listed as follows:

- Friends of a user
- Other nonfriend users of the OSN
- Advertiser(s)
- Cloud datacenters
- Certificate Authority
- Entities external to the OSN

As we stated earlier, we can assume that friends of a user are trusted entities, when it comes to the user's privacy. The other entities are analyzed next for the proposed system's vulnerability, considering them as threat agents.

5.2.1 *Other nonfriend users of the OSN and entities external to the OSN*

An adversary in these two categories needs to obtain the following information in order to breach a targeted user profile:

- At least k number of CDCs a user has subscribed to.
- Access information for all those k number of CDCs.

Let C be the complete set of CDCs that participate in the practical implementation of the proposed OSN, where $|C| \geq k, n$. A complete stranger who has no prior knowledge at all about the user's profile and his CDCs has no capability at all to identify the user's CDCs from C. Such an adversary needs to carry out a brute-force attack targeting all the CDCs in C to identify at least k number of CDCs the user has subscribed to, which is a nearly impossible task given the level of security commercial grade CDCs provide.

Therefore, the best chance such an attacker has is to penetrate into the Access Computer of the user or a friend of the user. In the proposed OSN, the friend network of a user is visible to a user only up to one tier, since we consider this as a privacy-related constraint that should be adhered to. In other words, a user cannot view friends of his friends and so on. Therefore, this type of adversary may not derive the information of friends of a target user through the OSN itself. The adversary will have to rely on other sources to gain such knowledge. Even with this knowledge, an adversary needs to penetrate into an Access Computer of a friend (or the user) to identify the user's CDCs and relevant authentication codes. Since Access Computers are not publicly available systems like CDCs and the Advertiser, we can safely assume that a user profile is immune to such an attack unless the adversary gets an opportunity to physically break into one of the Access Computers, and the level of the risk in such a threat depends on the system that got breached (a user's Access Computer or a friend's Access Computer). The adversaries may resort to social-engineering-based attacks to gain the necessary information from the user or his friends. Therefore, it is important for OSN users to follow the same precautionary measures taken to prevent other social-engineering-based attacks [48].

5.2.2 *CDCs*

Only the shares of user profiles are stored at CDCs and such a share of a profile does not reveal any information at all about a user's profile (even $(k-1)$ number of shares do not reveal anything about the user's profile, due to the properties of SSS). Ideally, a CDC does not know which other CDCs that the user has stored other shares of the profile at. Therefore, we can assume that the confidentiality of a user profile is protected from malicious CDCs or malicious inside parties of CDCs. Furthermore, unauthorized modification of profile shares by a CDC with the intention to alter a user's profile would simply make a meaningful reconstruction of the profile impossible with that profile share. In other words, when reconstructed, it will provide meaningless texts and unidentifiable images. Hence, the data integrity of a user's profile is preserved from a CDC. However, in cases where $n = k$ this would result in an attack on the availability of the user's profile. Simply ensuring that $n > k$ as a countermeasure would make the user's profile immune to such an attack.

A CDC needs to keep information about the friends of the user who are authorized to access his profile, in the access control DB and in the relation FRIENDS of the user's VPS (as shown in Figure 4.1). Therefore, a CDC is in a position to derive the social network graph for a user who has subscribed to its service, using unique identifiers for friends (e.g. email addresses) as the node identifiers. Although it will not directly reveal any other information about the friends (even their names), it reveals some important information such as how many friends the user has and how active the user is in the OSN (based on frequency of messaging, wall posting, and sharing content). Also, the list of email addresses of a user's friends is a good starting point for an adversary (a CDC or a malicious employee in a CDC) to dig for more information about friends. That kind of an attack can be made even easier when the majority of the friends have subscribed to the same CDC for the services of the OSN. In other words, if a particular CDC becomes prominent in the proposed OSN with a considerable number of users, it would be in a position to construct a good portion of the overall social network graph for the entire population of the OSN. However, we believe that this type of information does not pose a considerable threat to a user's privacy, and some precautionary measures from users and some mediation/standardization steps can avoid such information leakages.

5.2.3   *The Advertiser*

The Advertiser provides a global indexing service for all the OSN users to search for and add new friends, as explained in Chapters 3 and 4. Therefore, the Advertiser emulates certain functions of a central SNO. Even though the Advertiser does not store complete user profiles (only the public profiles of users are stored in the Advertiser) and is therefore not in a position to violate user privacy, there are some risks that need to be addressed. First, if we rely on only one Advertiser, then almost all the user connections will happen through that Advertiser. Therefore, the Advertiser can create and access the social network graph representing all the users in the OSN. This means that the Advertiser has access to the contact lists of all the users. However, as mentioned in Section 5.2.2, we believe that the contact list of a user is not that privacy sensitive when compared to other contents in an OSN environment, especially from the perspective of a relatively distant entity to the user such as the Advertiser and a CDC.

However, there are still two countermeasures that can be taken to overcome this risk, as follows:

- The proposed architecture can facilitate more than one Advertiser. At their own discretion, users can advertise themselves in more than one Advertiser. This way, a particular Advertiser might not be able to derive the complete social network graph for the whole OSN.
- The fundamental step in adding a friend in the proposed OSN is exchanging the header files containing information about the

CDCs between the user and a friend, as explained in Section 4.1.5. Such an exchange of header files can be done in secure ways other than through the Advertiser as well. For example, the user and the friend can exchange the encrypted header files through emails, or exchange them physically. Such an exchange in the context of the proposed OSN can be considered as "out-of-band". Adopting an out-of-band exchange for encrypted header files to add privacy-sensitive contacts can conceal them from the Advertiser(s).

The above-mentioned two counter measures avoid the risk of a central entity having access to the complete social network graph. Then an Advertiser would only be able to derive a portion of the social network graph of the OSN. Furthermore, the Advertiser would always fail to capture the removed edges resulting from removed friends, since such an activity does not occur through the Advertiser. Therefore, the derived social network graph may not be up to date.

5.2.4 *The Certificate Authority*

The CA provides two main functionalities: certifying users' digital security certificates that contain their public keys and maintaining a repository of such certificates. These X.509 certificates are the key for secure SSL/TLS sessions and the handshake protocol of adding friends as explained in Chapters 3 and 4. The CA is trusted only for these two basic tasks. Other than these two fundamental tasks, the CA is not involved in any of the functions in the OSN and no communications pertaining to the OSN occur through the CA. Therefore, we can safely assume that users' privacy in the OSN is secure from the CA.

5.2.4.1 *Can the users keep their own public keys and get the Advertiser to act as a mediator in the handshake protocol of adding friends?*

The CA and the Advertiser bring some centralization to the proposed OSN. However, it is important to decouple these roles into two entities. Keeping the public key of a user with the user himself and

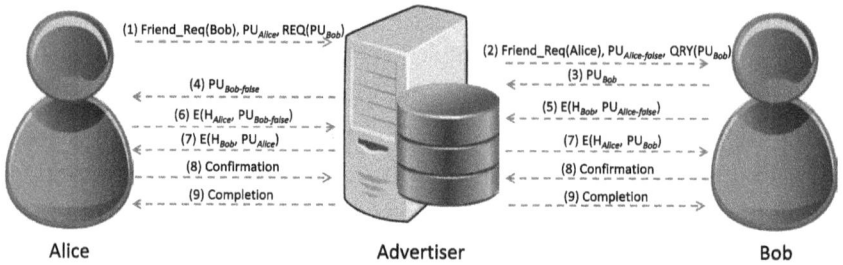

Fig. 5.1   Man-in-the-middle attack by the Advertiser, in the absence of a CA.

forwarding that to a friend through the Advertiser in the handshake protocol would make it possible to carry out a man-in-the-middle attack by the Advertiser, compromising the security of the whole OSN architecture. The following example illustrates that kind of an attack. Let us assume that Alice with the key pair (PR_{Alice}, PU_{Alice}) wants to add Bob with the key pair (PR_{Bob}, PU_{Bob}) as her friend. Since no CA is present, both users will have to query the other party's public key through the Advertiser. The Advertiser creates two pairs of false keys, one for each user as $(PR_{Alice-false}, PU_{Alice-false})$ and $(PR_{Bob-false}, PU_{Bob-false})$. Then during the handshake protocol, the communications would be as given in Figure 5.1, of which each step is outlined as follows:

1. With the friend request to Bob, Alice sends her public key (PU_{Alice}) to the Advertiser to be forwarded to Bob, while requesting Bob's public key (PU_{Bob}).
2. The Advertiser forwards Alice's friend request to Bob with $PU_{Alice-false}$, which is the falsely created public key for Alice by the Advertiser, and queries for PU_{Bob} from Bob.
3. Bob accepts Alice's friend request and sends PU_{Bob} to the Advertiser to be forwarded to Alice.
4. After getting PU_{Bob} from Bob, the Advertiser sends $PU_{Bob-false}$, which is the falsely created public key for Bob, to Alice.
5. Bob sends his header file containing access information to his CDCs after encrypting using $PU_{Alice-false}$. Now the Advertiser can decrypt it using $PR_{Alice-false}$.

6. Alice sends her header file containing access information to her CDCs after encrypting using $PU_{Bob-false}$. Now the Advertiser can decrypt it using $PR_{Bob-false}$.
7. The Advertiser now knows the access information to CDCs of both users. It now encrypts Alice's header file using PU_{Bob} and forwards it to Bob, and encrypts Bob's header file using PU_{Alice} and forwards it to Alice.
8. After getting the header files and adding the CDC access information for the friend in the Local_DB, both Alice and Bob confirm it to the Advertiser.
9. The Advertiser concludes the friend addition process between Alice and Bob.

From the steps mentioned in the man-in-the-middle attack, the Advertiser successfully obtains access information for all the CDCs along with proper authentication codes for both users. Thus, their privacy is compromised. Both users are unaware that such an attack actually occurred, in other words, it is passive in nature. Therefore, relying on Advertiser to act as a mediatory body while only users keep their own public keys carries a security risk. Thus, the role of the CA is significant in securing users' privacy in the proposed OSN architecture.

Table 5.1 compares the trust relationship model of the proposed OSN architecture with conventional OSNs and other proposed more secure alternative OSN architectures in different studies. A "Yes" means that the OSN architecture trusts the given entity when it comes to security and privacy of users, and a "No" is the opposite of the same fact. Some conventional OSNs provide some adjustable privacy controls for users. However, the users must adjust their privacy settings to get the desired level of security and privacy. Based on users' preferences or knowledge about such controls, the level of trust placed on external entities can vary from user to user. Therefore, such scenarios are represented with a "Yes and No". In conventional OSNs, the indexing service provider and the data storage provider are the same, i.e. the SNO, and by default the SNO is a trusted entity in

Table 5.1   Trust relationships in different OSN architectures.

Architecture	Friends	External Entities	Nonfriend OSN Users	Indexing Service Provider	Data Storage Provider(s)
Conventional OSNs	Yes	Yes and No	Yes and No	Yes, represents the SNO	
Anderson *et al.* [17]	Yes	No	No	Unknown	No
Shakimov *et al.* - Vis-'a-Vis [6]	Yes	No	No	Unknown	Yes
Baden *et al.* - Persona [34]	Yes	No	No	Unknown	No
Cutillo *et al.* - Safebook [26]	Yes	No	No	Unknown	Yes
Seong *et al.* - PrPl [45]	Yes	No	No	Unknown	Yes
Jahid *et al.* - DECENT [43]	Yes	No	No	Unknown	No
Buchegger *et al.* - PeerSoN [41]	Yes	No	No	Unknown	Yes
Aiello and Ruffo - LotusNet [27]	Yes	No	No	Unknown	No
Nilizadeh *et al.* - Cachet [44]	Yes	No	No	Unknown	No
Proposed Architecture	**Yes**	**No**	**No**	**No**	**No**

conventional OSNs. Other proposed alternative OSN architectures have not discussed providing an index service to search and add new friends. Some of them only discuss adding friends through out-of-band techniques. Therefore, for all other OSN architectures, the trust relationship with the indexing service providers is mentioned as "Unknown". Also, as in the proposed OSN, most conventional OSNs use SSL sessions for secure communications. However, other proposed OSNs that are listed in Table 5.1 have not identified mechanisms for secure communications, to be protected from eavesdroppers.

5.3   Security in Different Functionalities

In this section, the proposed architecture for the OSN is analyzed for its security in the primary operations and the secondary functionalities according to the security services defined in the X.800 standard [50], as applicable.

- **User registration:** The OSN application is installed with a username and a password chosen by the user to provide **access control** at the Access Computer level. The recommended minimum length of the authentication codes created by the OSN application is 128 bits (for both users and friends) to withstand a brute force attack (128 bits can create $2^{128} = 3.4 \times 10^{38}$ alternative authentication codes). A secure authentication code for a user provides **peer entity authentication, access control,** and **nonrepudiation, origin** security services when accessing CDCs.

- **Creating a user profile:** Only the user can initiate a command with WRITE access to the relations USER_INFO, EDUCATION, and WORK in the user profile DB in a user's VPS at a CDC. In order to provide such access control, the user is differentiated from other parties by the unique {email address, authentication code} pair of the user, in the HTTP POST request. Therefore, **peer entity authentication, access control** and **nonrepudiation, origin** security services are again achieved through the user's authentication code. The **connectionless confidentiality** of information of user profiles stored in CDCs is provided by secret sharing based encryption.

- **Accessing and updating a user profile:** The GK acts as a proxy when a user (or a friend) is accessing his profile DB in the allocated VPS of a CDC. To access a user's profile, the user requires READ permission to all the shares of his profile in all the VPSs in CDCs, and to carry out update operations on his profile he also needs WRITE permission (through the GK) to all the relations in the DBs in VPSs. Therefore, in the same way as in creating user profiles, the unique authentication codes (along with the email addresses) of users provide such **access control** along with **peer entity authentication** and **nonrepudiation, origin** security services.

- **Deleting a user profile:** Only the user has the access right to delete data in the VPSs for which the security services **access control, peer entity authentication** and **nonrepudiation, origin** are achieved through the user's authentication code. Requesting to discontinue the services from the CDCs can be made in person or in an agreed upon secure channel (e.g. a secure login for a CDC website).

- **Adding friends and contacts to the network**: Adding friends is achieved through the handshake protocol explained in Section 4.1.5. The **connectionless confidentiality** of header files is realized through RSA encryption of header files using a friend's public key. Also, **data-origin authentication, connectionless integrity** and **nonrepudiation, origin** security services are achieved by the RSA-based digital signature using a user's private key.

- **Removing friends and contacts from the network**: Removing a friend would result in deleting entries for that friend from the VISITORS relation in the access control DB and from the FRIENDS relation in the user's DB in the VPS. The GK would accept such a request only from a user. Here again **access control, peer entity authentication** and **nonrepudiation, origin** security services are realized by the user's unique {email address, authentication code} pair for each CDC.

- **Accessing friends' profiles**: As mentioned in Section 5.2.2, an unauthorized alteration of shares of a user profile would simply make the reconstructed profile data from that share meaningless, due to the properties of secret sharing. Also, users and friends are properly authenticated through their authentication codes when updating a user profile (friends can update relations that are related to wall posts and comments). Therefore, the proposed OSN provides **connectionless integrity** and **data-origin authentication** when friends access the user's profile. In other words, a friend can ensure that all the posts and information shared in the user's profile are posted by the authors/owners as shown, and have not gone through unauthorized alterations thereafter. Also, **access control** and **peer entity authentication** security services are achieved through the authentication codes assigned to friends.

- **Sharing information and content**: Only users are allowed to share content in the user's profile, i.e. the requests to write data into the relations ALBUMS, PHOTOS, VIDEOS and the relations mentioned under "creating user profile" are accepted only from the user, by the GK of a CDC. Again **access control, peer entity authentication** and **nonrepudiation, origin** security services are to be achieved through the user's authentication code when sharing information and content in his profile. Only the authorized users with correct authentication codes can access content shared by the user. The authentication codes are kept at CDCs as hash values of those authentication codes, rather than plain authentication codes. Therefore, an adversary inside a CDC does not have direct access to authentication codes. Furthermore, shares would not reveal any information about profile data as long as the number of shares accessible by an adversary is less than k. Thus, a CDC does not have access to a user's profile data. This means that the **connectionless confidentiality** of user profiles (and shared information and content) is accomplished in the proposed OSN architecture.

- **Wall posting and commenting on shared content**: Just as in accessing friends' profiles, **access control, peer entity authentication** and **nonrepudiation, origin** security services of wall posts and comments are to be realized through the authentication codes assigned to friends. Also, when viewing such wall posts and comments (by the user himself or by a friend), **connectionless integrity** and **data-origin authentication** are achieved due to the same reason, i.e. the {email address, authentication code} pair is unique to the user or a friend and no one else can make wall posts or comments on behalf of them or alter them in such a way to display a semantically different message. Just like in sharing information and content, only the authorized entities (user and friends) can view wall posts and comments, thus providing **connectionless confidentiality** to wall posts and comments.

- **Messaging**: When messaging, the friend's ID (email address) must match the authentication code provided to him. This provides **access control, peer entity authentication** and **nonrepudiation, origin** security services when the friend sends a message. The same mechanism ensures **data-origin authentication**,

connectionless integrity and **nonrepudiation, origin** security services when that message is later reviewed by the user. The GK provides READ access for messages only to the user. Thus, **connectionless confidentiality** is achieved in messages in the OSN, i.e. only the user and friend can view their message history, by accessing their own respective VPSs.

It is important to note that the **connection confidentiality** is achieved for all the primary operations and secondary functionalities through SSL/TLS sessions.

5.4   Security Against Identified Attacks

In Chapter 2, we discussed the spectrum of attacks in an OSN environment as presented in [21]. The resiliency of the proposed OSN architecture is analyzed against these attacks as follows:

- **Plain impersonation:** An adversary can still create a fake profile for a target real-world user in the proposed OSN if the adversary has access to valid information about the target user that uniquely identifies the user from others, e.g. full name, a profile photo that identifies the user, current city, date of birth, etc. Social-engineering-based attacks are a good source for such information about real-world users. As a countermeasure, the Advertiser and CDCs can put in place rigorous authentication (validation) mechanisms when a user registers for service, to ensure that the registered user is the person that he claims to be. However, such an authentication mechanism may reduce the flexibility and user-friendliness of the overall architecture.
- **Profile cloning:** As a special type of an impersonation attack, profile cloning relies on the OSN itself to provide valid information about the user to create the impersonated fake profile. In the proposed OSN, only the friends of the user are allowed to access the user's profile information. The friends are assumed to be trusted entities in the proposed OSN. Therefore, the proposed OSN is resilient against profile cloning. The only vulnerability is at the

Advertiser level, where an adversary can clone the public profile of the user at the Advertiser. Since cloning cannot go beyond that level, the probability of exposing the adversary is higher in such a situation, because the actual profile will reveal that the attacker is fake as soon as he is connected.

- **Profile porting:** In another type of an impersonation attack, an adversary doing profile porting gathers information about a target user in the OSN from another OSN. Even rigorous authentication mechanisms as mentioned under "plain impersonation" may fail under this kind of an attack. Therefore, the proposed OSN is vulnerable against profile porting. As a precautionary measure, users have to rely on privacy settings provided by other OSNs and must make sure all of their OSN profiles are secured from entities external to OSNs and other nonfriend OSN users. Also, an adversary cannot port a target user's profile information from the proposed OSN to another OSN, since the proposed OSN is secure from such adversaries as mentioned in Section 5.2.1.

- **Profile hijacking:** An adversary would only know of the existence of the target user's profile in the OSN through the Advertiser. Apart from that, the adversary does not have knowledge of which CDCs the user has stored his profile shares on. Even with such knowledge, the adversary has to obtain the authentication codes of the user to hijack the user's profile. Simple hacking techniques such as password guessing that have proved to be effective in attacks on real-world online applications (due to weak passwords), would not work in the proposed OSN as the authentication codes are created by the OSN application and not by the user and can be assumed to be strong. The only vulnerability arises when an adversary physically accesses the Access Computer and breaks into the OSN application of the user due to a weak password put in place by the user.

- **Profiling:** Profiling is impossible in the proposed OSN, as the user profiles are completely kept confidential from all other parties except for a user's friends. The only information a profiling attacker can gather is a user's public profile which carries much less information about the user that is considered by the user to be privacy insensitive.

- **Secondary data collection:** The collection of information about a user from secondary information sources is beyond the control of the OSN. However, successful prevention of profiling may hinder an adversary's effort to successfully find secondary information sources about the user. In other words, immunity against profiling attacks may create resiliency against secondary data collection, as secondary data collection is considered to be the second phase of a profiling attack.

- **Fake requests:** The proposed OSN is also vulnerable to fake requests, simply because the acceptance or otherwise of a friend request is solely decided by the user. While the user may not accept friend requests from unknown users of the OSN, they are highly vulnerable when the fake request is from a fake account created by a successful plain impersonation attack or a profile porting attack.

- **Crawling and harvesting:** The vulnerability to crawling and harvesting in the proposed OSN is limited to the information available in users' public profiles because users' actual profiles are kept confidential from all third-party entities. Therefore, the level of success of crawling and harvesting in the proposed OSN is low.

- **Image retrieval and analysis:** The proposed OSN is resilient against this type of an attack since all the contents shared by a user including images is kept confidential from third-party adversaries.

- **Communication tracking:** None of the external adversaries and nonfriend OSN users can track the communications of the user. Even a friend of a user can view only wall posts, comments on shared content, and the messages between the user and that particular friend. However, a CDC of a user can track the frequency of communications by the user and the frequency of communications of friends with respect to the user's profile, i.e. number of wall posts, messages, and comments a particular friend makes.

- **Fake profiles and Sybil attacks:** Fake profiles are still a threat in the proposed OSN, unless proper user validation mechanisms are introduced into the system. As mentioned under "fake requests", the proposed OSN does not shield users from Sybil attacks, and it is expected that users follow due diligence when accepting a friend request from another user.

- **Ballot stuffing:** The proposed OSN does not provide a platform to create public opinions or interests. Also, friends of a user are trusted and validated entities. Therefore, ballot stuffing is not a threat in the proposed OSN to create unfair public interests, to make users uncomfortable in their real lives, or to carry out a DoS attack in the OSN.

- **Defamation:** Assuming that friends are trusted, user profiles are immune to defamation attacks in the proposed OSN as user profiles are inaccessible beyond the tier of the user's friends, unlike in a conventional OSN. The only platform where all the users of the OSN are present collectively is at the Advertiser and it does not provide any functionality at all to users to express themselves. Therefore, the proposed OSN is completely resilient against defamation.

- **Censorship:** Due to the absence of a centralized SNO, the proposed OSN is protected from censorship at an SNO level. However, censorship can be present at group levels caused by a group moderator.

- **Collusion attacks:** Collusion attacks can be targeted at the Advertiser and at the CDCs. Assuming that the total number of CDCs in the OSN is adequate and none of the CDCs dominate the user accounts in the OSN, such a collusion attack on a single CDC may not hinder the functioning of the whole OSN. A successful collusion attack on the Advertiser will only jeopardize adding new friends, while the rest of the functions can still be carried out smoothly. A collusion attack targeted to damage a user (his reputation) is not possible as user profiles are not visible beyond their friends. Even with a collusion attack that successfully creates a fake account and gets connected to the user, the user's reputation is still protected as all contributions from friends to the user profile (e.g. wall posts, comments) need user approval before getting posted on his profile.

Table 5.2 Resiliency of the prosposed OSN against different attacks in an OSN environment.

Attack	Vulnerability
Plain impersonation	Vulnerable
Profile cloning	Safe
Profile porting	Vulnerable
Profile hijacking	Safe
Profiling	Safe; Such an attack is only possible at the level of the user's public profile
Secondary data collection	Less vulnerable due to immunity against profiling
Fake requests	Vulnerable
Crawling and harvesting	Safe, and only vulnerable up to users' public profiles
Image retrieval and analysis	Safe
Communication tracking	Safe, and only vulnerable to the extent of leakage of information to CDCs, pertaining to how frequent the communications are
Fake profiles and Sybil attacks	Vulnerable
Ballot stuffing	Safe
Defamation	Safe
Censorship	No censorship at an SNO level; Censorship is still possible at group levels by group moderators
Collusion attacks	Safe; However, a successful DoS attack to the Advertiser can block adding new friends

Table 5.2 summarizes the above analysis of the proposed OSN architecture against different attacks that are identified in [21]. As a note of comparison, it is important to note that the conventional OSNs Facebook© and LinkedIn© are vulnerable to all the attacks mentioned in Table 5.2.

5.5 Vulnerability Assessment Against Known Cloud Security Risks

CDCs are a major component of the proposed OSN architecture. Shares of user profiles are stored in CDCs and are expected to be secure from unauthorized access. However, CDCs also face security risks of their own, which in turn can affect the overall security of the proposed OSN architecture. In this section, we discuss whether the proposed OSN is vulnerable to such risks, or whether the inherent properties of the proposed OSN circumvent such risks. Stallings and Brown [51] provide a list of known technical cloud security risks presented in [8], [30], and [49] that we use as a framework in our analysis, considering those risks one by one as follows:

- **Abuse and nefarious use of cloud computing:** Refers to attacks carried out by malicious external users once they are allowed to access the cloud infrastructure for legitimate services. If such an attack occurs, the attacker can breach confidentiality as a passive attack, or actively try to alter data stored or jeopardize the service availability by that particular CDC. However, in the context of the proposed OSN, the confidentiality of user profile data will still be preserved as only the shares of user profile are stored in the VPS in the CDC and those shares do not reveal any information at all about the original secret profile. The attacker may still obtain the list of friends (only by their email addresses) of all the users who have subscribed to that particular CDC. The integrity of the user profile will still be preserved as unauthorized modifications of the profile data would simply make the reconstruction of the profile semantically meaningless (as explained in Section 5.2.2). If $n > k$ in the threshold scheme adopted for secret sharing by the user, then the availability of the user's OSN profile will not be affected in case the attack caused the services from the CDC to become unavailable.

- **Insecure interfaces and APIs:** If a security breach occurs through an interface in the CDC that is not relevant to the proposed OSN, the above-mentioned arguments under "Abuse and nefarious use of cloud computing" still hold true when it comes to the security and privacy of the OSN users. The only interface of a CDC in the context of the OSN is the GK. The GK implements proper authentication and access control mechanisms as explained in Chapters 3 and 4, along with secure verified communications through SSL/TLS sessions. Other security mechanisms such as activity monitoring can be incorporated by the CDC administration on the GK to provide additional security. Therefore, we can safely assume that the external interface of a CDC with respect to the proposed OSN is adequately secure.

- **Malicious insiders:** The same arguments as presented under "Abuse and nefarious use of cloud computing" apply for malicious insiders at CDCs, and we can expect that the privacy of users and profile data integrity will stilll not get affected by malicious insider attacks. Furthermore, the fact that authentication codes are only stored as hash values improves the security of the system against such attacks.

- **Shared technology issues:** The underlying hardware components of a CDC may not be designed to offer strong isolation properties that are essential in a CDC environment. The CDC administration may approach this issue by using isolated virtual machines for individual clients. This approach is argued to be vulnerable to both insider and outsider attacks. Since this threat is just another risk that provides opportunity for inside and outside adversaries, the discussion made under "Abuse and nefarious use of cloud computing" and "Malicious insiders" is valid for this scenario as well.

- **Data loss or leakage:** For most general CDC clients, this has the most devastating impact in a CDC security breach. However, the OSN users do not have to worry about data leakage as their profiles are already encrypted by secret sharing, and a single share does not reveal any information at all about actual profile data. However, trivial information about users' profiles such as number of friends, and number of wall posts, albums, photos, videos, messages, etc., still may get leaked in such a security breach. Data loss would not impact the OSN user profiles as long as $n > k$ in the threshold secret sharing scheme that the user has adopted. Therefore, it is always recommended for users to select a value for n such that $n > k$, for greater availability.

- **Account or service hijacking:** This is one of the top threats in CDC environments. Usually, stolen credentials are a main source for such attacks. In the proposed OSN, the effects of such an attack in the context of a single CDC are negligible as explained under "Data loss or leakage", as long as the number of the user's CDCs where account hijacking has occurred is less than or equal to

$n - k$. Then the user can inform the CDC administration about the attack and take necessary steps to rectify the issue. However, if the number of CDCs that the account hijacking has occurred in is more than $n - k$, then data loss is a risk, if the attacker actively vandalizes shares of the user's profile. If the number of CDCs that the account hijacking has occurred in is more than or equal to k, then data leakage is also an imminent threat. Therefore, it is of paramount importance that users keep their access credentials safe (such as authentication codes) from all potential adversaries.

- **Unknown risk profile:** This is a risk that arises from users ceding control of their data to CDCs. There are primary expectations from the CDCs in the proposed OSN, such as not to work with other parties (e.g. other CDCs) to breach the privacy of OSN users. Such expectations can be made legally binding. Also, there are secondary expectations that impact the security of the overall architecture of the OSN, such as CDCs exercising necessary access control and authentication mechanisms. These expectations need to be standardized and agreed upon by the CDC when the user registers for services. This way, the threats due to the unknown risk profile of CDCs can be managed and minimized in the proposed OSN architecture.

5.6 Summary

In this chapter, we discussed why SSS is a good candidate for encrypting user profiles before storing them in multiple CDCs as shares of the original secret profile. The capability to provide information theoretic security, the flexibility to support the dynamic nature of social networks, the high availability, and the low risk of exposing user profiles to CDCs are the main justifications for choosing secret sharing over conventional data encryption algorithms. The proposed architecture protects the confidentiality and the integrity of user profiles from other nonfriend users of the OSN, the Advertiser(s), CDCs, the CA, and entities external to the OSN. However, a CDC of a user can derive certain information about the user such as number of contacts of the user and the level of activities of the user within the OSN. Also, if only a single Advertiser is present in the OSN, it can derive the complete social network graph of the OSN, though it may not be up to date. The importance of the CA to protect the handshake protocol of adding new contacts from man-in-the-middle attacks by the Advertiser was also discussed in this chapter. Primary operations and secondary functionalities of the proposed OSN were analyzed for their security, considering the X.800 standard as a framework. The proposed OSN is resilient against most of the attacks that are present in a conventional OSN. However, there is still some vulnerability against plain impersonation, profile porting, fake profiles and Sybil attacks, and fake requests. The proposed OSN is also immune to threats that are considered as risks in cloud computing environments, especially due to the inherent properties of SSS.

Chapter 6

Feasibility, Performance, and Scalability Analysis

Chapters 3 and 4 provided a blueprint-level description of the proposed secure and privacy-aware cloud-based architecture for online social networking. Going further we wanted to observe the feasibility of using SSS in the context of an OSN and how the user interactions in such an OSN will be. Therefore, we implemented a proof of concept (POC)-level execution of the proposed architecture in a lab environment. Section 6.1 explains the objectives of the POC implementation as well as what was not covered, along with the network setup of the POC implementation. Section 6.2 presents the results of the POC testing. The proposed OSN is analyzed for its performance in Section 6.3, and is further analyzed for its scalability in Section 6.4.

6.1 Scope of the POC Implementation

The main objectives of this experimentation were as follows:

- To test whether the proposed methods of using SSS in multimedia encryption (as explained in Chapter 3) are applicable in an OSN environment as proposed in this study. In this implementation, we have considered only text and image secret sharing. We believe video secret sharing needs more research, especially in the compressed domain, before being applied in an OSN environment.

- To measure and get an early insight into the added overhead in processing time in the proposed OSN architecture due to multimedia secret sharing.

- To check whether the proposed architecture can support in creating user friendly interfaces for users to interact with, given the fact that it is an essential feature in OSNs and given that the proposed system introduces numerous security features and an architecture that an average user may not be that familiar with. However, it is important to note that the focus was not on the design of the GUI, but to test the functionality.

Therefore, the implementation in the lab environment was not a full-fledged implementation of the OSN architecture as presented in Chapters 3 and 4, as it was intended to meet the above-mentioned objectives. The experimental implementation was limited in scope when compared to the full model explained in Chapters 3 and 4 as follows:

- No TLS/SSL sessions were used in the experimental setup as we believe it is standard and can be easily incorporated into the system. Also, we assumed the Advertiser to be a trustworthy entity to the extent that it will not carry out a man-in-the-middle type of attack (as discussed in Chapter 5). However, we still wanted the header files to be exchanged after being encrypted using the RSA algorithm using users' public keys. Therefore, in this implementation users can transfer their public keys through the Advertiser before exchanging the header files. Due to these two reasons there was no CA present in this implementation.

- All the CDCs and the Advertiser were implemented in one DB server.

- Since the number of users involved in testing is very low (just two users), we had only one DB for each CDC to accommodate all the users and their profile data, i.e. there were no multiple VPSs in this implementation, on the basis of one VPS per each user.

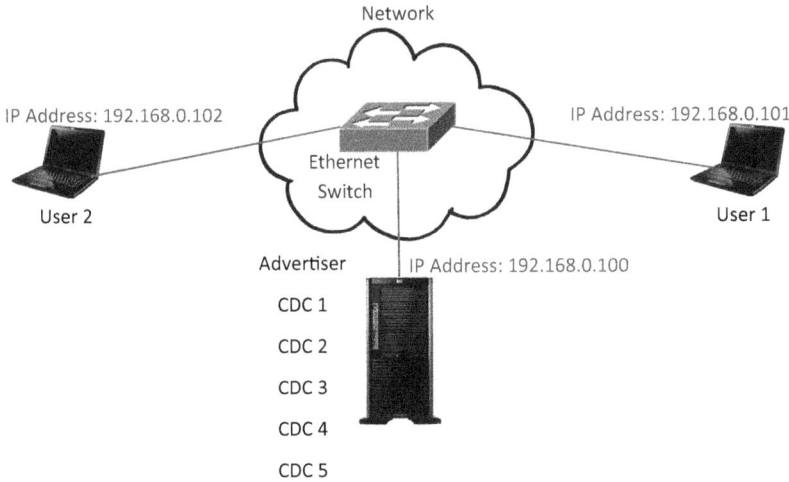

Fig. 6.1 System setup for the POC implementation.

- Not all the fields of the relations shown in Figure 4.1 were implemented as some of them were not required in this simplified implementation version of the proposed OSN.

We used a $(3, 5)$ threshold scheme for secret sharing in the experimental setup; hence, we used 5 CDCs in the implementation. The system setup for the POC implementation is shown in Figure 6.1. Here, all three computing devices are in the same local area network $(192.168.0.0/24)$. The network cloud is simply an Ethernet switch connecting the three devices. In an actual OSN scenario, the network cloud would be much more complex.

6.2 Feasibility Analysis

According to the objectives mentioned in Section 6.1, the following functions were tested in the POC implementation.

1. Creating a user profile.
2. Sharing content in a user profile.
3. Accessing a user profile.

4. Searching for friends and adding friends to the user's network.
5. Accessing a friend's profile.
6. Wall posting on a friend's wall.

The resulting graphical user interfaces along with test inputs are shown for each of the above functions as applicable. Also, when it is relevant, the changes in the DB entries are also shown for the functions mentioned above.

6.2.1 *Creating a user profile*

Figure 6.2 shows a sample GUI of a user inputting his profile information when creating his profile. Figure 6.3 shows a resulting entry in the relation USER_INFO in the DB of a CDC. It displays the shares that are created for all the profile data elements including the profile picture, except for the Email as explained in Chapter 4.

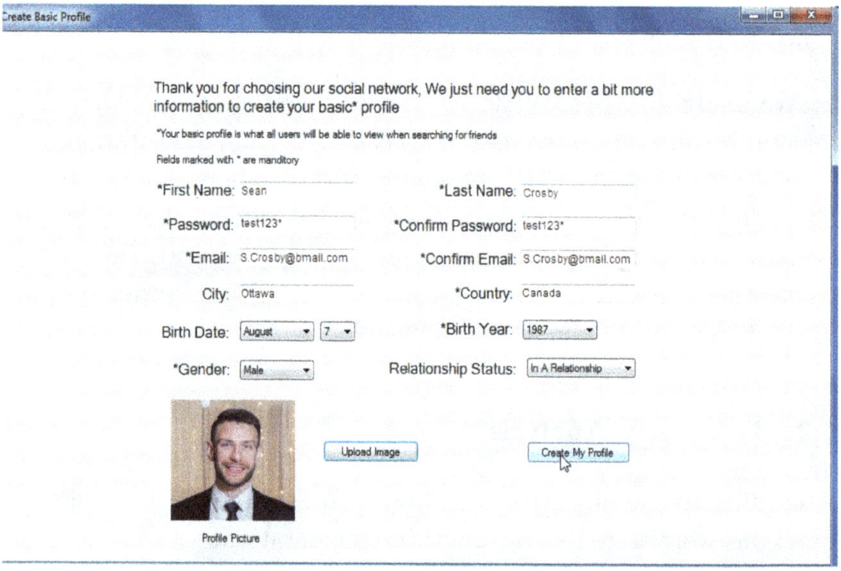

Fig. 6.2 GUI for creating a user profile.

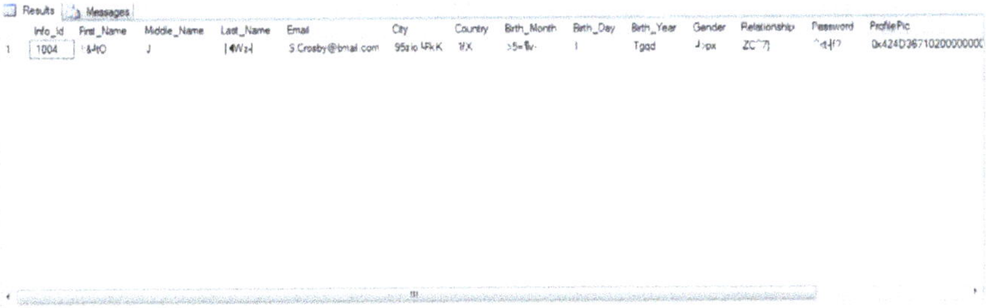

Fig. 6.3 DB entry in a CDC for the created user profile.

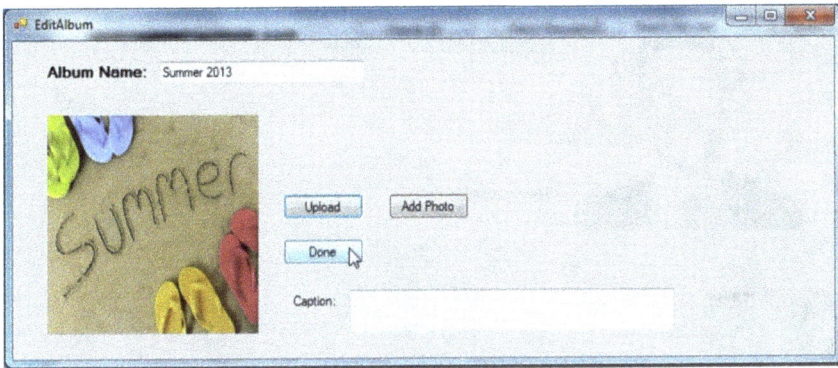

Fig. 6.4 GUI for creating an album and sharing a photo.

6.2.2 *Sharing content*

As an example of sharing content, we considered creating an album and uploading a photo to the same album. Figure 6.4 depicts the GUI window for uploading a photo to the album named "Summer 2013". Figure 6.5 shows the corresponding DB entries in the relations ALBUMS and PHOTOS of a CDC.

6.2.3 *Accessing user profile*

In this experiment, the user logs into his profile and views the photo albums in his profile and the photos in one of the albums. Figure 6.6

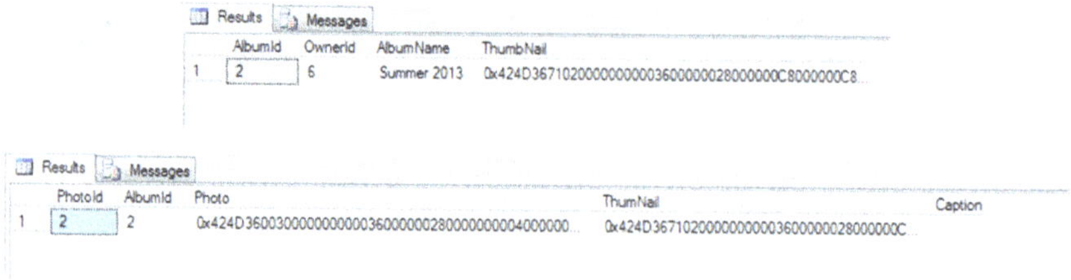

Fig. 6.5 DB entries in a CDC for the created album and shared photo.

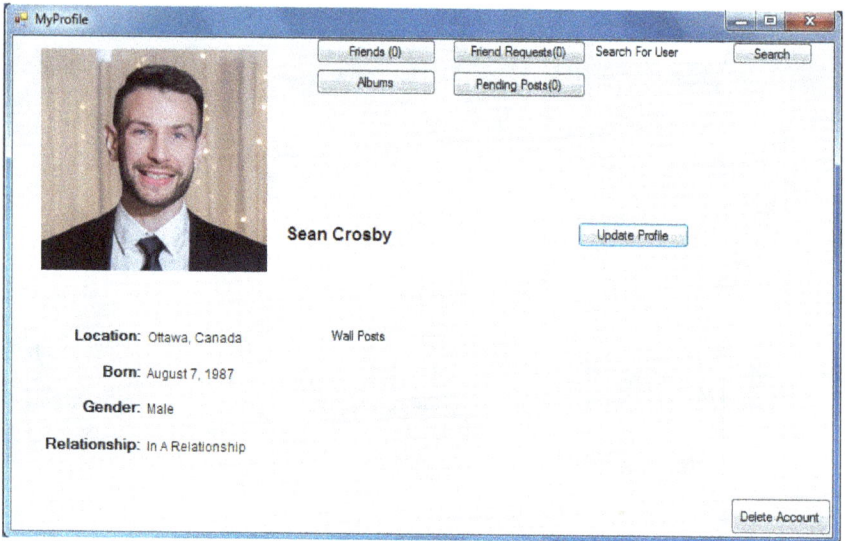

Fig. 6.6 GUI for user's own profile homepage view.

shows an example homepage view when a user accesses his own profile. Figures 6.7 and 6.8 are GUI windows for displaying the photo albums and photos of an album, respectively.

6.2.4 *Searching for and adding friends*

As for the test of searching for friends, the user "Sean Crosby" searched for another user named "Sam Nadella" in the OSN. The search results are shown in Figure 6.9, with the expected legitimate

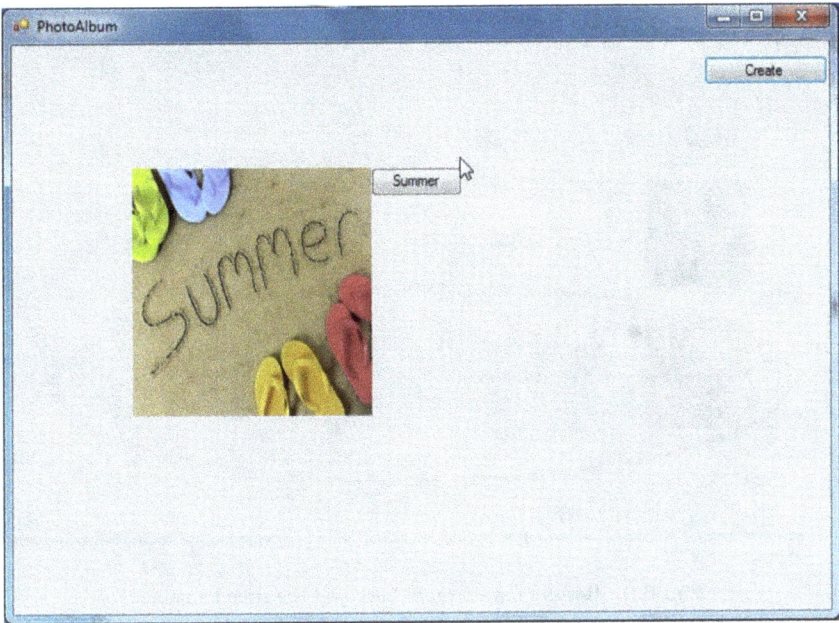

Fig. 6.7 GUI for viewing of photo albums.

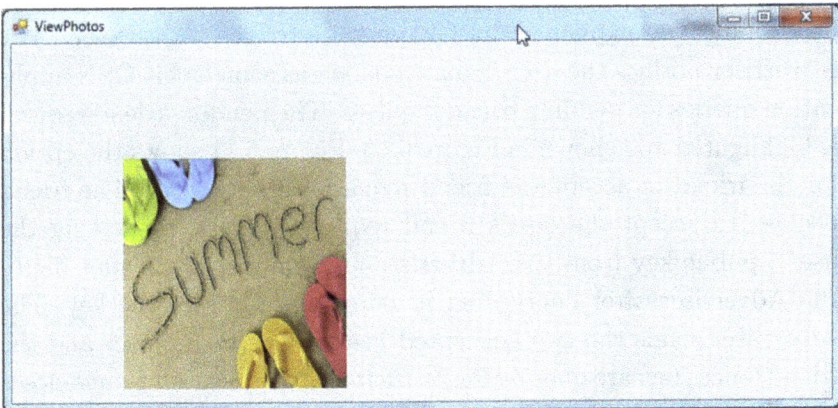

Fig. 6.8 GUI for viewing individual photos.

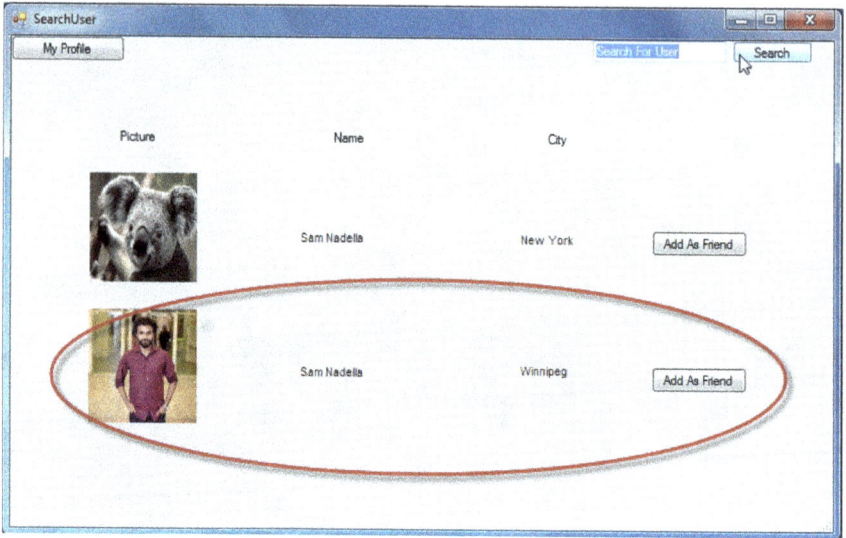

Fig. 6.9   Results for a search, based on the friend's name.

user along with a fake user (or another user with the same name as the friend). The expected user is highlighted in the figure. The user decides to add the legitimate user as his friend, then requests the friend's public key from the Advertiser and sends the encrypted header file (as explained in Chapter 4) to the Advertiser. The Advertiser notifies the user "Sam Nadella" as soon as his OSN application queries for pending friend requests. The pending friend request is highlighted and shown in Figure 6.10. Figure 6.11 shows the option for the friend to accept the friend request from the user. The friend decides to accept the user's friend request, thereby requesting the user's public key from the Advertiser and sending his header file to the Advertiser after encrypting it using the user's public key. The Advertiser sends the two encrypted header files to the user and the friend, once they are queried for by their OSN applications, and closes the friend request by flagging the entry it created for this friend request as shown in Figure 6.12 (in the column "RequestAccepted").

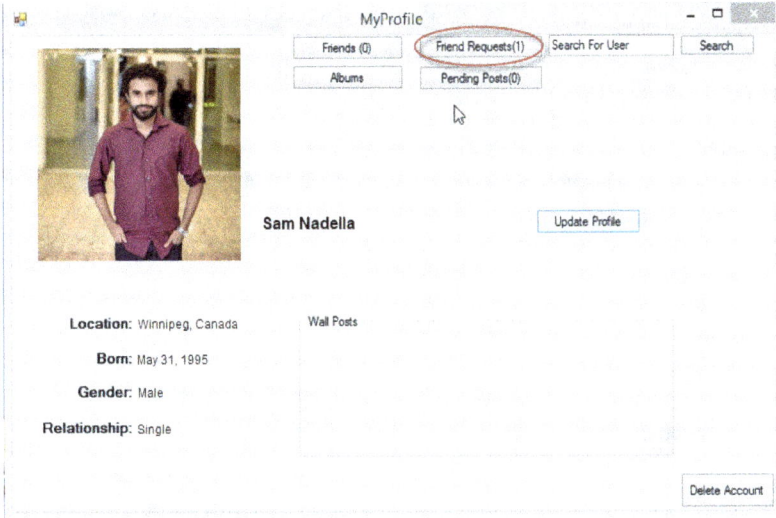

Fig. 6.10 Indication of a pending friend request.

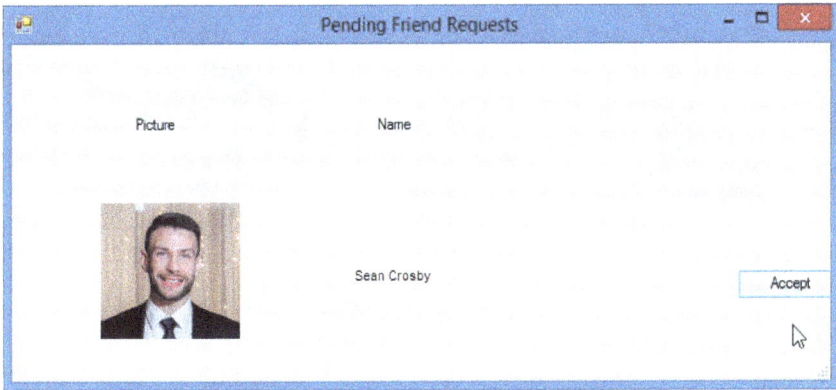

Fig. 6.11 Pending friend request to be accepted.

Fig. 6.12 An entry at the Advertiser for a successfully completed friend request.

6.2.5 *Accessing a friend's profile*

When accessing a friend's (in this case the friend is Sean Crosby) profile, the user just has to select the friend of interest from the list of friends and view his profile homepage first, as shown in Figure 6.13. The resulting GUI window of the friend's profile homepage is shown in Figure 6.14. Once the user accesses the friend's homepage, he may navigate to other profile information of the friend (e.g. photos), as he wishes.

6.2.6 *Wall posting*

As shown in Figure 6.14, a friend's profile homepage view provides an input text field to post textual messages on a friend's wall. As explained in Chapter 4, a wall post needs the profile owner's approval before being displayed on his wall. When the user posts a message on his friend's wall, the user receives a notification indicating the need for the friend's approval. Such a notification along with the wall post written by the user (highlighted) is shown in Figure 6.15.

The CDCs notify the friend of pending wall posts, as explained in Chapter 4. Such a notification in the friend's OSN application GUI is shown in Figure 6.16 (highlighted), which is followed by Figure 6.17, which shows the wall post GUI window prompting the friend's acceptance. Figure 6.18 displays the friend's new profile homepage with the

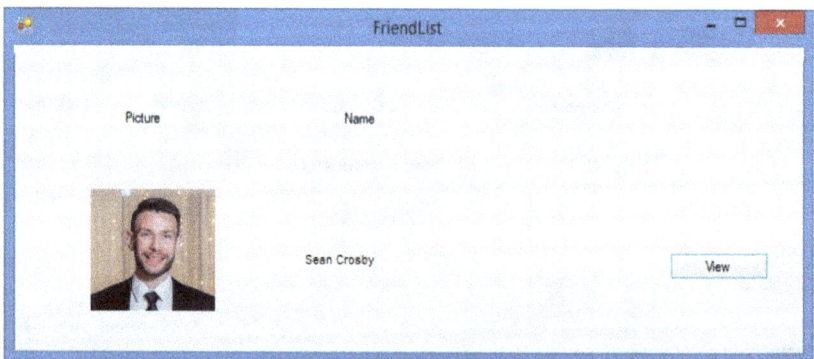

Fig. 6.13 GUI view of the list of friends of a user.

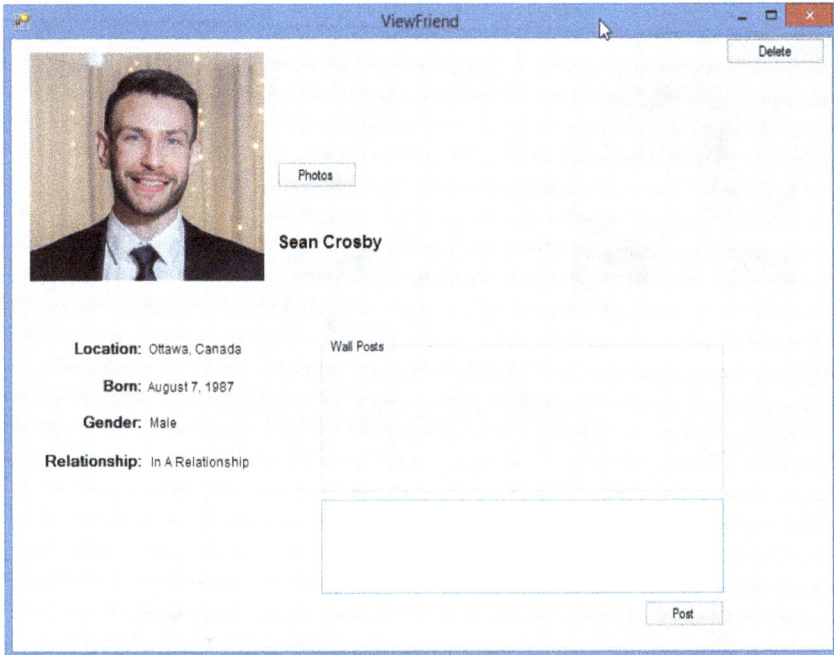

Fig. 6.14 User profile view from a friend's point of view.

new wall post, after he accepted it. Figure 6.19 illustrates the entry for a share of a wall post in the relation WALL_POSTS in a CDC before and after it was accepted by the friend. The field "Accepted" was FALSE (0) before the friend accepted it, and it was changed to TRUE (1) once it was accepted.

6.3 Performance Analysis of the Proposed OSN

In the proposed architecture, the main additional processing overhead comes from creating shares of a secret when uploading, and revealing the secret from k number of shares when downloading, compared to a conventional OSN. We measured the complete time it took to upload different images and texts to CDCs after creating n number of shares, and the time it took to reconstruct them with k number of shares, in the implementation shown in Figure 6.1. In the proposed

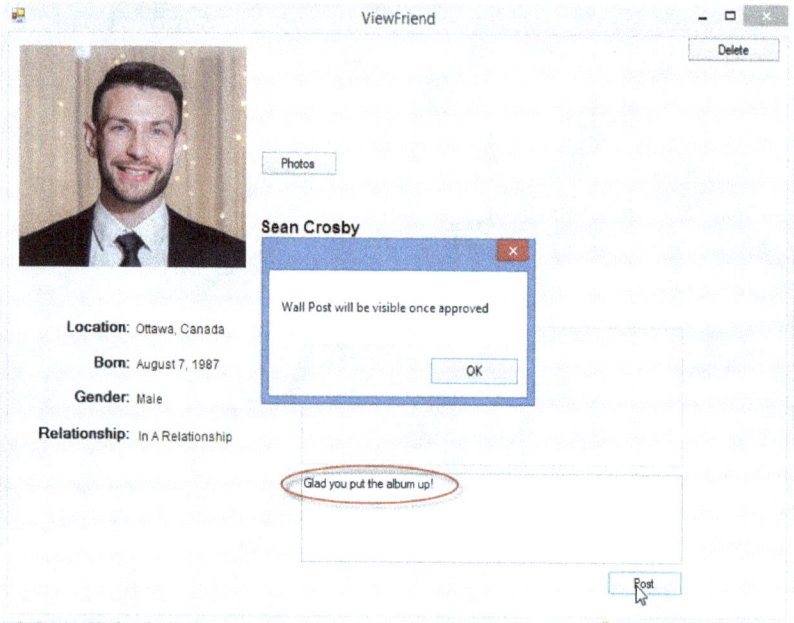

Fig. 6.15 A wall post created on a friend's profile with the message notifying the need for friend's approval.

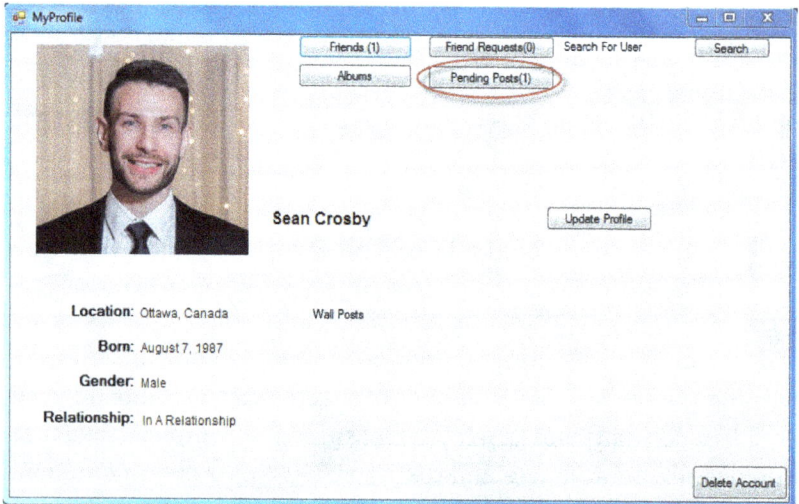

Fig. 6.16 Pending wall post notification on friend's profile.

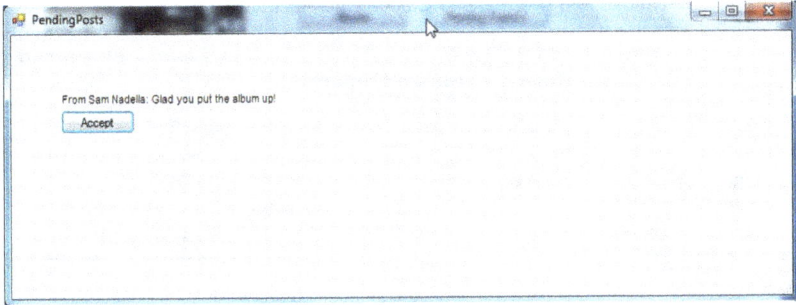

Fig. 6.17 The wall post from user to friend with the option of accepting it.

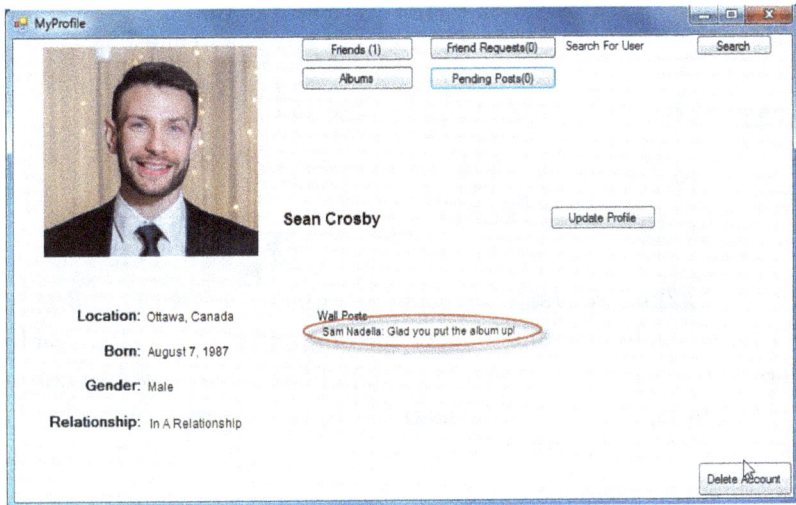

Fig. 6.18 Accepted wall post being displayed on the friend's profile with the name of the author of the wall post.

Fig. 6.19 DB entries in the relation WALL_POSTS in a CDC before and after approving a wall post.

Table 6.1   Upload and download times for different images in the proposed OSN.

	Image Format	Image Size	Image Dimensions	Upload Time	Download Time
Image 1	JPEG	373 kB	1024 × 768 = 786432	14.612 s	12.442 s
Image 2	BMP	768 kB	512 × 512 = 262144	7.885 s	6.619 s
Image 3	BMP	527 kB	600 × 600 = 360000	6.176 s	4.219 s
Image 4	JPEG	1.24 MB	1774 × 1182 = 2096868	17.782 s	14.926 s
Image 5	BMP	6 MB	1183 × 1774 = 2098642	16.141 s	12.907 s

Table 6.2   Upload and download times for different texts in the proposed OSN.

	No. of Characters in the Text	Upload Time	Download Time
Text 1	6	2.269 s	1.602 s
Text 2	18	2.420 s	1.865 s
Text 3	48	3.284 s	1.765 s
Text 4	171	3.741 s	2.770 s
Text 5	285	4.216 s	2.742 s

OSN, uploading refers to creating n number of shares and transmitting them to n number of cloud datacenters, and downloading refers to requesting and receiving k number of shares from k number of cloud datacenters and reconstructing the secret profile data. As mentioned earlier, in this implementation $k = 3$ and $n = 5$. Measured uploading and downloading times for different images and character strings are given in Tables 6.1 and 6.2. Images were uploaded and downloaded as photos, and texts were uploaded and downloaded as wall posts, in the context of the proposed OSN.

Upload and download times of texts were relatively consistent, as seen in Table 6.2. However, there were considerable variations when it came to upload and download times of images (Table 6.1). For example, Images 4 and 5 took comparatively longer times to be uploaded and downloaded. This is due to the fact that the size (as well as the resolution) of these images are comparatively large.

Most conventional OSNs resize large images before storing them. Resizing large images such as Images 4 and 5 before uploading them may reduce the processing time in uploading and downloading in the proposed OSN.

Referring to Tables 6.1 and 6.2, it is clear that the processing overhead is relatively higher for images. This is because the number of pixel values is usually much higher than the number of characters in a text string. In an image, the number of pixels is the main factor affecting the number of operations in creating shares and reconstructing the secret, whereas in texts it mainly is the number of characters in the text that affects the number of operations. Due to this reason, we will focus on uploading and downloading images in the proposed OSN, compared to conventional OSNs.

Let T_{con} be the time delay in a conventional OSN to upload and download an image (assuming it is the same for both operations), and let $T_{Tx_{\text{con}}}$ be the transmission-related time delay in the network between the client device and the OSN server. Assuming that there is no pre-processing required in conventional OSNs when uploading (and downloading) an image,

$$T_{\text{con}} = T_{Tx_{\text{con}}} \tag{6.1}$$

Let T_{up} and T_{down} be the total time delays in uploading and downloading an image in the proposed OSN, respectively. Let T_{ss} and T_{sr} be the time it takes to create shares and reconstruct the image, respectively. Let T_{Tx} and T_{Rx} be the total network time delays in transmitting all the n number of shares to CDCs and receiving k number of shares from CDCs, respectively. Then,

$$T_{\text{up}} = T_{ss} + T_{Tx} \tag{6.2}$$

$$T_{\text{down}} = T_{sr} + T_{Rx} \tag{6.3}$$

Let the secret-sharing threshold scheme adopted be (k, n). Then all the secret-sharing schemes for digital images presented in

Section 2.4.2 create shares of the same size of I/k, where I is the size of the image to be encrypted, in number of pixels. Assuming the network bandwidth from the client to the OSN server in a conventional OSN scenario and the network bandwidth from the Access Computer to all the CDCs to be the same,

$$T_{Tx} = T_{Tx_{\text{con}}} \times n/k \tag{6.4}$$

$$T_{Rx} = T_{Tx_{\text{con}}} \tag{6.5}$$

From Equations (6.1–6.3),

$$T_{\text{up}} = T_{ss} + (n/k) \times T_{\text{con}} \tag{6.6}$$

$$T_{\text{down}} = T_{sr} + T_{\text{con}} \tag{6.7}$$

If the value n/k is not significantly larger than 1 (e.g. for $n = 5$, $k = 3 \Rightarrow n/k = 1.67$), we can conclude that both T_{up} and T_{down} are dominated by T_{ss} and T_{sr}, respectively. This is especially true for higher bandwidth internet connections, where T_{con} is relatively low. When considering this fact with Table 6.1, we can conclude that the time delays in the proposed OSN are at an acceptable level, considering the added level of privacy it provides. Furthermore, the time delay in uploading an image in a conventional OSN may be relatively high as well (in that case the assumption that the upload time and the download time are the same is no longer valid as well as Equation (6.1)). This is due to the pre-processing of images before they get uploaded to the server at the SNO. As an example, Table 6.3 shows the upload and download times in Facebook© for the same images listed in Table 6.1 over a residential Internet link of 10 Mbps.

Table 6.3 Upload and download times for the same images as in Table 6.1, in Facebook©.

	Upload Time	Download Time
Image 1	12.16 s	<1 s
Image 2	10.93 s	<1 s
Image 3	8.36 s	<1 s
Image 4	14.74 s	<1 s
Image 5	35.95 s	<1 s

6.4 Scalability Analysis

When discussing how the proposed OSN can meet the demand for future expansions, we can assume that the CDC operators can increase the resources allocated for user data storage as the demand increases. Therefore, the two main bottlenecks to be considered in the proposed OSN, when it comes to its scalability, are:

1. OSN transaction processing at Access Computers.
2. Communications and request processing (mainly at GKs) at CDCs.

The average number of friends per user in an OSN environment can be considered to be around a few hundred. As an example, the median friend count on Facebook© is around 100, as of November 2011 [1]. Therefore, we believe that a simple lightweight database management system such as SQLite© (an open-source, self-contained, server-less, zero-configuration SQL database engine) [3] or XML-based data storage would be sufficient to manage LOCAL_DB at Access Computers. Furthermore, concurrent processing of the OSN application is not required as the OSN application will only be processing one transaction at a time. Owing to these reasons we believe the expansion of OSN users would not necessitate an increase of processing power and storage requirements at Access Computers.

However, with the increase of the number of users in the OSN, more users may subscribe to CDCs to host shares of their profile data. This may demand more processing at GKs and concurrent communication links at the CDCs. To address the problem of resource limitation at GKs, a CDC administration can adopt a bank of GKs rather than a single GK, where a single GK would front end a cluster of VPSs. Such a configuration is shown in Figure 6.20. In that case, each CDC would require a "Redirector" to front end the communications from OSN users. The redirector would simply forward requests to the matching GK for further processing.

An optimized solution would be to have a load balancing mechanism among all the GKs of a particular CDC. In that case, the

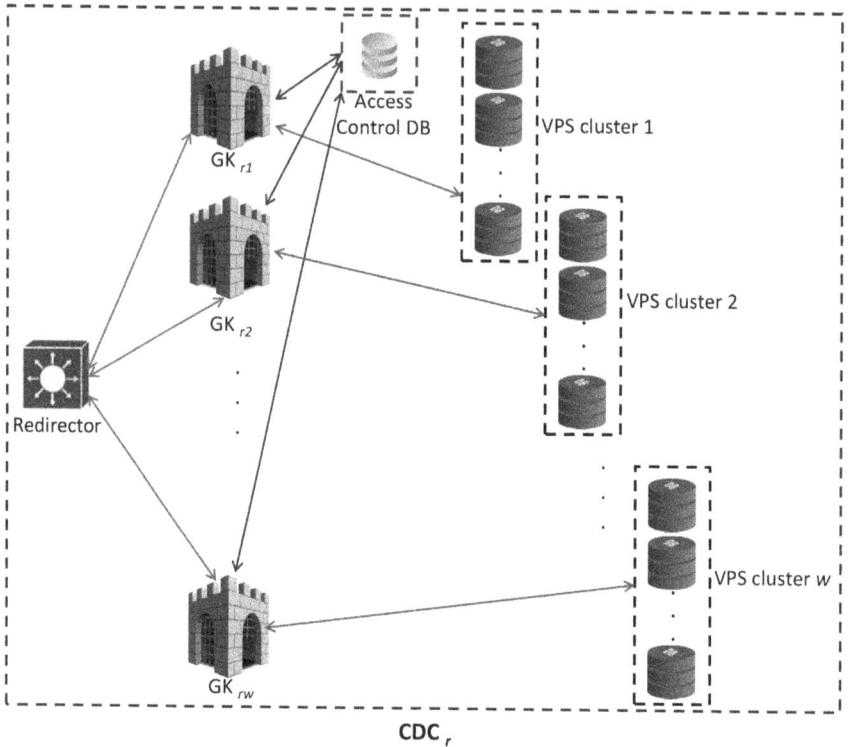

Fig. 6.20 Multiple GKs supporting clusters of user VPSs to support increased processing demand at CDCs.

redirector would make the decision of where to forward requests and queries from users and their friends, based on the current processing load of all the GKs. Then the ratio of the number of network connections between GKs and VPSs would be $w : v$ (w is the number of GKs and v is the number of user VPSs, at a particular CDC), rather than $1 : 1$. Then the corresponding network topology within a CDC would be as illustrated in Figure 6.21.

Although multiple GKs can solve the bottleneck of processing demands at CDCs, another limiting factor can be the number of external concurrent network connections a CDC can provide. To handle such a demand, just like many other commercial-grade CDCs and conventional OSNs, the CDCs can provide multiple public IP

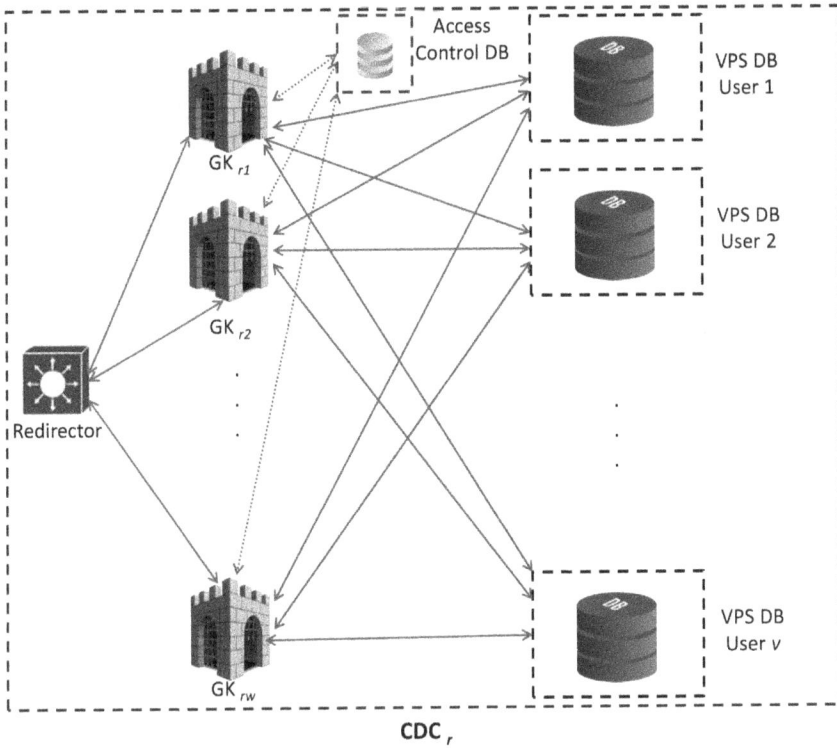

Fig. 6.21 A load balancing configuration for multiple GKs.

addresses. This means multiple redirectors will have to front end at the CDC, and redirect user requests to GKs based on their current load of processing. Having a URL to represent the CDC rather than a set of fixed IP addresses can increase the flexibility of the overall architecture. The same URL can act as the unique CDC ID. In that case, users and friends need access to a DNS server that can resolve the URL to a correct IP address. Such a requirement is not very taxing as users (and friends) usually have access to a DNS from their respective Internet Service Providers (ISPs). Figure 6.22 depicts this flexible topology. The ability of a CDC to evolve as the demand for its service increases as explained above shows that the proposed architecture can potentially scale with its growth.

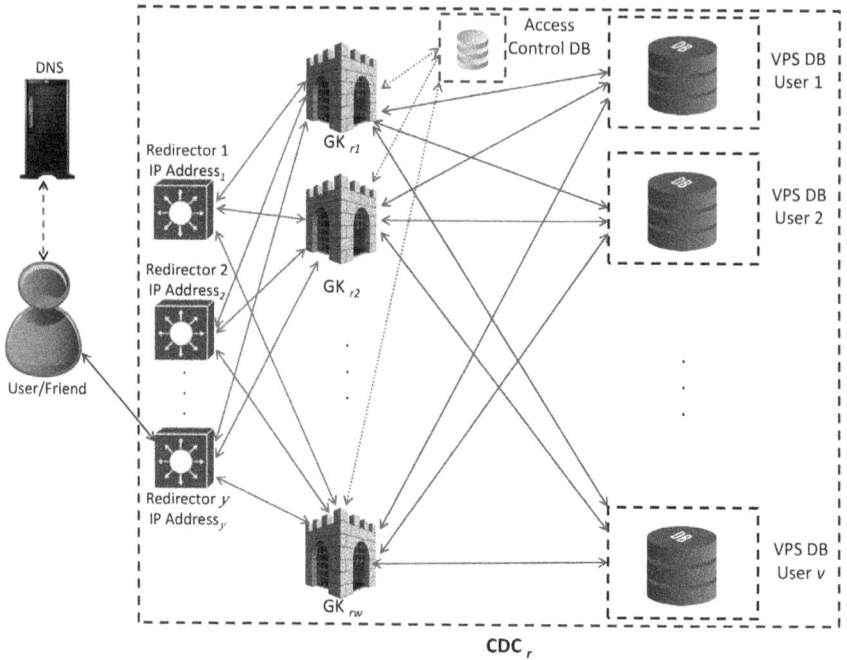

Fig. 6.22 Accommodating multiple IPs for users/friends to access a CDC.

6.5   Summary

This chapter presented the details of a POC implementation of the proposed OSN, starting with the scope of the implementation. Creating a user profile, sharing content in a user profile, accessing a user profile, searching for friends and adding friends, accessing a friend's profile, and posting on a friend's profile wall were the operations and functionalities that were tested in the POC implementation. The results of the tests done on the POC implementation were presented and then analyzed for the performance overhead that the proposed OSN introduces when compared to conventional OSNs. The proposed OSN is flexible enough to adapt to the increasing resource demand when the number of users increases, and thus it is a scalable architecture.

Chapter 7

Conclusions and Future Works

In this chapter, we summarize the presentation of this book along with its concluding remarks, which is presented in Section 7.1. We believe that this study is just the beginning and only a framework for a more secure and privacy-aware online social networking user experience. More focused research attempts may be used to optimize and develop this framework further. Section 7.2 provides an overview of such possible research directions for the proposed OSN architecture.

7.1 Concluding Remarks

OSNs have become an effective means of mapping existing real life social networks to an online domain, maintaining them, and extending them further. They are also rich sources of user interaction applications such as instant messaging and gaming. However, despite such strengths, users' awareness about issues of privacy of personal information in conventional centralized OSNs is increasing. In particular, securing user privacy from SNOs is getting more and more attention from regulatory bodies, scholars, and users.

There have been several studies proposing solutions in existing OSNs to protect user privacy from potential adversaries, including SNOs. Mainly due to an anticipated lack of support from SNOs to implement such solutions, researchers have proposed completely new architectures for OSNs. While there have been several new architectures that follow the same client–server model as conventional OSNs, a significant portion of the researchers who have worked on this relatively novel research domain believe that the solution lies in complete decentralization. They believe that the centralization of user profiles is the main risk in an OSN environment. Most of such research works suggest that migrating OSNs to peer-to-peer layers is the best form of decentralization. Some scholars believe that hosting user profiles on virtual individual servers may bring the required decentralization to OSNs.

In this book, we presented a decentralized architecture (SecureC-Social) for online social networking based on distributed secure storage of user profiles in multiple CDCs, with SSS as the method of encryption. SSS is considered to be information theoretically secure and the intention was to bring the robustness of such an encryption algorithm to the security of user profiles in the OSN. The CDCs, the Advertiser(s), the CA, and Access Computers are the major system components of the proposed OSN architecture. All the communications between these entities are carried out on SSL/TLS sessions, thus providing protection from eavesdroppers. On top of the high level of information security provided by SSS, the rigorous information security mechanisms put in place by commercial grade CDCs provide an additional layer of security to user profiles along with high availability. The proposed OSN is also open to any multimedia secret-sharing algorithm as long as it is accepted as a standard throughout the whole OSN.

User registration, creating a user profile, accessing and updating a user profile, deleting user profiles, adding contacts to the friend network, removing friends, and accessing friends' profiles are considered to be the basic primary operations in an OSN environment. This book has provided an in-depth presentation on how the proposed OSN architecture can perform all those primary operations along with the secondary functionalities of searching for contacts according to different criteria, messaging, sharing information and content, wall posting, and commenting on shared content. Our work provides details about the access control and authentication mechanisms in place to ensure confidentiality, integrity, and availability of user profiles. The achievement of all the above-mentioned primary operations and secondary functionalities can be realized based on simple relational databases. Representative relational database schemas are also presented in this book. The explanations of the primary operations and secondary functionalities are complemented by sample SQL commands and/or queries as applicable. This further supports our argument on the feasibility of the proposed architecture for an OSN.

Enhanced security and privacy of users is the main research goal of this book. Therefore, we analyzed the proposed OSN for its security from multiple perspectives. The proposed OSN considers users' friends as the only trusted parties in its trust relationship. Thus, the proposed OSN is analyzed for its security, considering other nonfriend users and external entities, the Advertiser(s), CDCs, and the CA as different threat agents. The proposed OSN is capable of preserving confidentiality, integrity, and availability of user profiles, and most of the functionalities of the OSN in the face of an attack from these threat agents. The proposed architecture is analyzed to identify any security vulnerabilities when primary operations and secondary functionalities are performed. In this book, we have shown that all such operations and functionalities are secure against all the active and passive attacks, considering the security services defined in the X.800 standard as a framework. Next, the proposed OSN is analyzed to determine how secure it is against known risks and attacks in an OSN environment. It shows resiliency against most of such attacks while still showing some vulnerability against plain impersonation, profile porting, fake requests, fake profiles, and Sybil attacks. This book has also revealed that it can provide immunity against threats and risks known to exist in cloud computing environments, thus ensuring that the use of CDCs does not become a vulnerability itself in the proposed OSN. One important concluding remark is that it is always recommended for users to select a value for n such that $n > k$ for higher availability (in a (k, n) threshold scheme for secret sharing).

As a final research goal, this book has provided a feasibility analysis of the proposed OSN with a proof of concept implementation of the same. It proved that the proposed OSN architecture can be implemented smoothly as outlined in this book with the discussed primary operations and secondary functionalities. Most importantly, it provided an indication that the additional computational overhead introduced by SSS is not too taxing on the OSN, and the system performance is at an acceptable level. The proposed OSN architecture also shows strong scalability features thus providing space for potential future expansions of the OSN with more users.

7.2 Future Works

The proposed architecture is just a framework for an OSN. There is much room for future improvements and evolution in the form of adding more functionality and optimizing the proposed framework. One such functionality of interest would be "Identity Management", where access rights are set for friends in a much finer granularity. We believe that creating and maintaining a Discretionary Access Control (DAC) matrix would be a strong candidate as a solution. Furthermore, the proposed architecture is open to other functionalities such as tagging user-shared content and other future functionalities that other OSNs may implement. We believe the proposed architecture can be optimized for better performance in communication overhead and processing time.

While the proposed OSN architecture is analyzed for its security in this research from multiple perspectives, doing security analysis from other different perspectives can be helpful in locating loopholes in the security mechanisms in the OSN, which can be an asset in similar systems that use secret sharing and secret reconstruction as the encryption and decryption methods, respectively, when storing data and retrieving it. When a particular share in a CDC is compromised and modified by an adversary, it is important for the user to know that such an attack has occurred and in which CDC it has occurred.

This aspect is a potential future optimization in the security of the proposed OSN.

Extending the proposed architecture to multiple access devices is another important area of future works. This basically involves synchronizing the OSN application instances of multiple access devices including the instances of LOCAL_DBs.

References

1. Anatomy of facebook©, available at `https://www.facebook.com/notes/` `facebook-data-team/anatomy-of-facebook/10150388519243859` (Accessed on June 2014).
2. Facebook© statement of rights and responsibilities, available at `https://` `www.facebook.com/legal/terms/` (Accessed on August 2013).
3. Sqlite©, available at `http://www.sqlite.org/` (Accessed on June 2014).
4. Richter A. and Koch M. Functions of social networking services. In *8th International Conference on the Design of Cooperative Systems*, pp. 87–98, Provence, France, 2008.
5. Shakimov A., Varshavsky A., Cox L.P., and Caceres R. Privacy, cost, and availability tradeoffs in decentralized OSNs. In *2nd ACM workshop on Online Social Networks*, pp. 13–18, Barcelona, Spain, 2009.
6. Shakimov A., Lim H., Caceres R., Cox L.P., Li K., Liu D., and Varshavsky A. Vis-à-vis: Privacy-preserving online social networking via virtual individual servers. In *3rd International Conference on Communication Systems and Networks*, pp. 1–10, Bangalore, India, 2011.
7. Shamir A. How to share a secret. *Communications of the ACM*, 22(11): 612–613, 1979.
8. Cloud Security Alliance. Top threats to cloud computing v1.0. Technical Report, 2010.
9. Krishnamurthy B. and Wills C.E. Characterizing privacy in online social networks. In *1st ACM workshop on Online social networks*, pp. 37–42, Seattle, Washington, USA, 2008.
10. Lin C.-C. and Tsai W.-H. Secret image sharing with capability of share data reduction. *Optical Engineering*, 42:2340–2345, 2003.
11. Thien C.-C. and Lin J.-C. Secret image sharing. *Computers & Graphics*, 26(5):765–770, 2002.
12. Chen D. and Zhao H. Data security and privacy protection issues in cloud computing. In *The International Conference on Computer Science and Electronics Engineering 2012*, pp. 647–651, Hangzhou, China, 2012.
13. Rescorla E. *RFC2818-HTTP Over TLS*. Network Working Group, Internet Engineering Task Force, 2000.
14. Steel E. and Vascellaro J.E. Facebook, myspace confront privacy loophole. *The Wall Street Journal*, 2010.

15. Toch E., Sadeh N. M., and Hong J. Generating default privacy policies for online social networks. In *28th ACM International Conference on Extended Abstracts on Human factors in Computing systems*, pp. 4243–4248, Atlanta, Georgia, USA, 2010.

16. Krawczyk H. Secret sharing made short. *Springer Lecture Notes in Computer Science*, 773:136–146, 1994.

17. Anderson J., Diaz C., Bonneau J., and Stajano F. Privacy-enabling social networking over untrusted networks. In *2nd ACM Workshop on Online Social Networks*, pp. 1–6, Barcelona, Spain, 2009.

18. Jonsson J. and Kaliski B. *RFC3447-Public-Key Cryptography Standards (PKCS) No. 1: RSA Cryptography Specifications Version 2.1*. Network Working Group, Internet Engineering Task Force, 2003.

19. Staddon J. Finding "hidden" connections on linkedin, an argument for more pragmatic social network privacy. In *2nd ACM workshop on Security and Artificial Intelligence*, pp. 11–14, Chicago, Illinois, USA, 2009.

20. Senevirathna K. and Atrey P.K. A secure and privacy-aware cloud-based architecture for online social networks. In *7th Multi-Disciplinary International Workshop on Artificial Intelligence*, pp. 223–234, Krabi, Thailand, 2013.

21. Cutillo L.A., Manulis M., and Strufe T. Security and privacy in online social networks. In F. Furht, (Ed.), *Handbook of Social Network Technologies and Applications*, pp. 497–522, Springer, Heidelberg, 2010.

22. Cutillo L.A., Molva R., and Önen M. Safebook: A distributed privacy preserving online social network. In *2011 IEEE International Symposium on a World of Wireless, Mobile and Multimedia Networks*, pp. 1–3, Lucca, Italy, 2011.

23. Cutillo L.A., Molva R., and Strufe T. Leveraging social links for trust and privacy in networks. *IFIP Advances in Information and Communication Technology*, 309:27–36, 2009.

24. Cutillo L.A., Molva R., and Strufe T. Privacy preserving social networking through decentralization. In *6th International Conference on Wireless On-Demand Systems and Services*, pp. 133–140, Snowbird, Utah, USA, 2009.

25. Cutillo L.A., Molva R., and Strufe T. Safebook: A privacy-preserving online social network leveraging on real-life trust. *IEEE Communications Magazine*, 47(12):94–101, 2009.

26. Cutillo L.A., Molva R., and Strufe T. Safebook: Feasibility of transitive cooperation for privacy on a decentralized social network. In *3rd IEEE World of Wireless, Mobile and Multimedia Networks Workshop on Autonomic and Opportunistic Communications*, pp. 1–6, Kos, Greece, 2009.

27. Aiello L. M. and Ruffo G. Lotusnet: Tunable privacy for distributed online social network services. *Computer Communications*, 35:75–88, 2012.

28. Lucas M.M. and Borisov N. Flybynight: Mitigating the privacy risks of social networking. In *7th ACM Workshop on Privacy in the Electronic Society*, pp. 1–8, Alexandria, Virginia, USA, 2008.

29. Raju N., Ganugula U., Srinathan K., and Jawahar C.V. A novel video encryption technique based on secret sharing. In *15th IEEE International*

Conference on Image Processing, pp. 3136–3139, San Diego, California, USA, 2008.

30. European Network and Information Security Agency. Cloud computing: Benefits, risks and recommendations for information security - enisa report. Technical Report, 2009.

31. Atrey P.K. A secret sharing based privacy enforcement mechanism for untrusted social networking operators. In *3rd International ACM Workshop on Multimedia in Forensics and Intelligence*, pp. 13–18, Scottsdale, Arizona, USA, 2011.

32. Atrey P.K., Hildebrand K., and Ramanna S. An efficient method for protection of text documents using secret sharing. In *International Conference on Frontiers of Computer Science*, Bangalore, India, 2011.

33. Atrey P.K., Alharthi S, Hossain M.A., AlGhamdi A., and El Saddik A. Collective control over sensitive video data using secret sharing. *Springer International Journal of Multimedia Tools and Applications*, August, published online, 2013.

34. Baden R., Bender A., Spring N., Bhattacharjee B., and Starin D. Persona: An online social network with user-defined privacy. In *ACM SIGCOMM 2009 Conference on Data Communication*, pp. 135–146, Barcelona, Spain, 2009.

35. Fielding R., Irvine U. C., Gettys J., Mogul J., Frystyk H., Masinter L., Leach P., and Berners-Lee T. *RFC2616-Hypertext Transfer Protocol – HTTP/1.1*. Network Working Group, Internet Engineering Task Force, 1999.

36. Alharthi S. and Atrey P.K. Further improvements on secret image sharing scheme. In *2nd ACM Workshop on Multimedia in Forensics, Security and Intelligence*, pp. 53–58, Firenze, Italy, 2010.

37. Alharthi S. and Atrey P.K. An improved scheme for secret image sharing. In *2010 IEEE International Conference on Multimedia and Expo (ICME)*, pp. 1661–1666, Suntec City, Singapore, 2010.

38. Alharthi S., Atrey P.K., and Kankanhalli M.S. Secret video sharing. In *APSIPA Annual Summit and Conference 2010*, Biopolis, Singapore, 2010.

39. Bhadravati S., Khabbazian M., and Atrey P.K. On the semantic security of secret image sharing methods. In *IEEE Seventh International Conference on Semantic Computing*, pp. 302–305, Irvine, California, USA, 2013.

40. Buchegger S. and Datta A. A case for p2p infrastructure for social networks - opportunities and challenges. In *6th International Conference on Wireless On-demand Network Systems and Services*, pp. 161–168, Snowbird, Utah, USA, 2009.

41. Buchegger S., Schiöberg D., Mittal P., Vu L.H., and Datta A. Peerson: P2p social networking: Early experiences and insights. In *2nd ACM EuroSys Workshop on Social Network Systems*, pp. 46–52, Nuremberg, Germany, 2009.

42. Guha S., Tang K., and Francis P. Noyb: Privacy in online social networks. In *1st Workshop on Online Social Networks*, pp. 49–54, Seattle, Washington, USA, 2008.

43. Jahid S., Nilizadeh S., Mittal P., Borisov N., and Kapadia A. Decent: A decentralized architecture for enforcing privacy in online social networks. In *4th International Workshop on Security and Social Networking*, pp. 326–332, Lugano, Switzerland, 2012.

44. Nilizadeh S., Jahid S., Mittal P., Borisov N., and Kapadia A. Cachet: A decentralized architecture for privacy preserving social networking caching. In *8th International Conference on Emerging Networking Experiments and Technologies*, pp. 337–348, Nice, France, 2012.

45. Seong S.W., Seo J., Nasielski M., Sengupta D., Hangal S., Teh S.K., Chu R., Dodson B., and Lam M.S. Prpl: A decentralized social networking infrastructure. In *1st ACM Workshop on Mobile Cloud Computing & Services: Social Networks and Beyond*. Article No. 8, San Francisco, California, USA, 2010.

46. Bhuiyan T., Josang A., and Xu Y. Managing trust in online social networks. In F. Furht, (Ed.), *Handbook of Social Network Technologies and Applications*, pp. 471–496. Springer, Heidelberg, 2010.

47. Dierks T. and Allen C. *RFC2246-The TLS Protocol Version 1.0*. Network Working Group, Internet Engineering Task Force, 1999.

48. Thornburgh T. Social engineering: The "dark art". In *1st Annual Conference on Information Security Curriculum Development*, pp. 133–135, Kennesaw, Georgia, USA, 2004.

49. Jansen W. and Grance T. Guidelines on security and privacy in public cloud computing. Technical Report, National Institute of Standards and Technology, 2011.

50. Stallings W. *Cryptography and Network Security, Principles and Practice — Fifth Edition*. Prentice Hall, 2011.

51. Stallings W. and Brown L. *Computer Security, Principles and Practice — Second Edition*. Prentice Hall, 2012.

Index